After Alice

Building a Foundation to Preserve the Land

Alice Ferguson and her Berkshire hogs

A Memoir by

Kay Gardner Powell

Kay Powell

After Alice: Building a Foundation to Protect the Land

ISBN 978-1-7342644-0-1

First Printing December 2019

For permissions, contact:

kgardnerpowell@gmail.com

"A community is the mental and spiritual condition of knowing that the place is shared, and that the people who share the place defined and limit the possibilities of each other's' lives. It is the knowledge that people have of each other, their concern for each other, their trust in each other, the freedom with which they come and go among themselves."

~Wendell Berry

Table of Contents

PROLOGUE

When I drive down Bryan Point Road to my home in the Moyaone Reserve in Accokeek, Maryland, I sometimes think about what it would look like if Alice Ferguson had not bought Hard Bargain Farm in 1922. I have lived here for more than 50 years and Bryan Point Road is still a narrow, two-lane, forested back road leading to the Potomac River shoreline, only ten miles from Washington, D.C.

Accokeek still has many of the qualities of a small town, while other neighborhoods this close to the river are sometimes riddled with unsightly suburban development. I realize that part of my neighborhood's good fortune was that no one seemed interested in this isolated part of Southern Maryland in the 1920s, 30s, 40s or even well into the 50s after the war.

The first electricity didn't arrive until 1937. The winding journey here through little villages on Livingston Road wasn't replaced by the two-lane Indian Head Highway until 1950. Supermarkets were miles away. As city dwellers searching for a country retreat, Henry and Alice Ferguson chose this refuge in Accokeek long before those amenities arrived.

Alice Ferguson died in 1951 and three years later the Alice Ferguson Foundation was created in her memory. In 1979, twenty-eight years after Alice had passed, I became the second executive director of the foundation. I served as such for 20 years. From the beginning of this amazing experience I have felt a strong connection to Alice.

Many times, I have wished I could convey to her all the special and wonderful things that have occurred because of her settling here long ago. I thought about writing to Alice after all, she doesn't even know about the foundation. In fact, I did write many 'Dear Alice' letters but I quickly realized the problems associated with delivering those letters! Nevertheless, I have always felt this strong connection, because every day for 20 years I went to my office in the farmhouse that she had built at Hard Bargain and it wasn't a sterile cubicle on the top floor of an office building. Rather, at Hard Bargain I was surrounded by her paintings, her carefully chosen furniture, and memorabilia from her travels. I even used the dishes on which she and Henry dined. Alice had passed more than twenty years before I entered the scene in 1968, but in many ways, she was still present.

The people that Alice and Henry attracted became the early residents of the Moyaone Reserve. They had a sturdiness about them that made them unafraid of carving out a place for their families on five acres of land in an isolated location. I've heard tales of commuting to their jobs in Washington, D.C. by boat, a time a corporation tried to purchase large tracts of land for the establishment of an oil tank farm on the river across from Mount Vernon, and of neighborhood feuds over the creation of the Piscataway Park.

The biggest part of my story concerns the Alice Ferguson Foundation. My position as executive director allowed me to meet many of Alice and Henry's friends and others that followed them to Accokeek. When creating the Alice Ferguson Foundation, Henry wanted Alice's legacy to be enjoyed by the community and as executive director that function became part of my job.

Alice's book, *Adventures in Southern Maryland*, tells the stories of the early residents of the Moyaone Reserve - a tiny group of friends that played at the farmhouse, helped Alice with her archeology, and with projects that contributed to the war effort. Her book is still available for sale from the Alice Ferguson Foundation. I recommend reading it so that you can get a sense of those early days at Hard Bargain.

My memoir is about people who took the baton and joined with a small staff to create an award-winning environmental education program, an annual Potomac River Cleanup, and model partnerships with the National

Park Service and local school systems. And, of course, my own struggles and triumphs over the years as I learned to manage what Alice had created.

Alice Ferguson set the stage for us. I would like to think that somehow this memoir will reach her consciousness. I want her and others to know how her beloved Hard Bargain became our playground for more wonderful adventures.

Here it is, Alice. My account dedicated to you and to those who carried on with your work.

Kay Gardner Powell

November 2019

CHAPTER 1

Hard Bargain Farm

Alice Ferguson was an extraordinary woman who has become somewhat of a legend in Accokeek and the surrounding Washington, D.C. area. In her nearly 30 years as owner and hostess of Hard Bargain Farm, she created a community which has preserved thousands of acres along the Potomac.

Alice was an admiral's daughter and an artist who studied at the Corcoran Art Gallery. Her husband Henry was a graduate of the Harvard Class of 1905 and a classmate of Franklin D. Roosevelt. Henry's profession as a geologist required him to make frequent trips out west.

Alice and Henry lived in a city apartment on California Street in Washington, D.C. And though city life was enjoyable, both were eager to occasionally escape to something more natural on weekends and other free times. They had been searching for 10 or more acres in the country and in December 1922 their search led them to a 140-acre parcel of land and a rundown farm house in Accokeek, Maryland.

Although the property was truly larger than they had been looking for, the beautiful view of the Potomac River from the hilltop captured Alice's heart.

Perhaps her restlessness for more space, and her independence learned in childhood, spurred her on to purchase Hard Bargain Farm – on her own and while Henry was away on business. In his book, *Hard Bargain Adventures* written after Alice's death, Henry wrote:

> *"When I arrived home just before New Year's I enquired how the search for real estate was progressing. Alice, for once in her life embarrassed, confessed that Hard Bargain was such a beautiful place that she had signed the sales contract and made a deposit of one hundred dollars."*

Henry did not approve because he felt that he could not simultaneously be a field geologist and a country squire but he agreed to the purchase on condition that Alice would assume entire management of the place – and he would appear only as a guest! Alice lived up to the agreement, so when visiting Hard Bargain, one must remember that this was entirely Alice's doing. She showed us what can happen when we show love and devotion to the land and its people.

As the executive director of the foundation I was often asked "Where did this beautiful place get the name Hard Bargain"? Alice tells us in her book.

> *"All old Maryland places have names and we knew that ours must have one too, but the real estate agent ignored all questions. When we signed the deed, we saw it for the first time. We were the owners of Hard Bargain. It is rather a nice name after you get used to it, but it is no name to use when you take apples to market.*
>
> *About 1800 someone had only dower rights (widow's share for life of husband's estate) to the farm but sold it just the same. In the course of time the unlucky purchaser found he did not own the place and had to buy it again."*

Hence, he named it Hard Bargain. The farm soon became a wonderful country home, where friends gathered on weekends for gardening, volleyball, swimming in the river, and cocktails. Alice also discovered and documented an archeological site on the riverfront that later became a national historic landmark. And she helped with the establishment of a firehouse in the community.

The little country abode's influence expanded when Alice bought surrounding woodland for development into five-acre home sites, enticing friends to settle nearby. The colony (as it was referred to by Alice and Henry) became the Moyaone Reserve.

Following a long struggle with emphysema, Alice passed away in 1951. When she died, the little settlement was still in its infancy with 30 landowners and only 10 residents. Though Henry had become completely immersed in the doings of the settlement, his hands-off management declaration made early in their life created a dilemma. What was to become of Hard Bargain? They had no heirs. The closest thing to their hearts was Hard Bargain and the lovely little colony of friends.

Henry really was concerned about the community and wanted to do the right thing, respecting all that Alice had created. There was one little non-profit in the colony, the Bonds Retreat Water Company. Bonds Retreat was the first tract of land to be settled in the community. With Alice's help this organization was established to supply water from a community-shared deep well. It served the first residents and the primary leaders within the colony.

Henry's idea was to leave Hard Bargain to this water company. At a meeting of the Bonds Retreat Water Company, conducted at Hard Bargain's amphitheater in July 1952, there was extensive discussion of what to do next. A temporary planning committee was formed. The members were Charles Wagner, William Harris, Lee Fairley, Richard Kenah, Robert Straus, and Marshall Newman. Lee Fairly, a resident and chairman of the little non-profit stated,

> *"The water company had formally accepted the offer (to take the farm). The board was meeting with a lawyer to discuss changes to the charter and transfer of assets."*

It was time to decide how to manage the Hard Bargain estate and what projects might be of benefit to the community. Another resident, William Harris stated,

> *"... the colony has to face the possibility of Hard Bargain passing into other hands, but Fergie (Henry's nickname) is offering a unique mechanism by which all can be drawn together and providing a way of retaining the spirit of the community."*

Residents who knew Henry told me that he was overwhelmed by the responsibilities of running the farm. He was ready to relinquish ownership and accept life tenancy at Hard Bargain as long as Saturday cocktails continued.

A planning committee was formed to gather ideas and propose a possible structure for the Bonds Retreat Water Company that would include ownership of the farm. There was great passion and concern among the residents and Henry was prepared to deed the whole of Hard Bargain to this group. The minutes of a meeting of the Bonds Retreat Water Company in March 1953 noted:

> *"We would all like to see Hard Bargain continue just as it is, as a farm, with all its associations. But in view of the annual cost of upkeep, the prospect of a lot of us white collar workers trying to run it as a successful operation seems to make that impossible. Yet, if it doesn't have cattle on it, it will grow up to brush in no time."*

The discussion continued on what projects and uses could make keeping Hard Bargain as Alice had so thoughtfully developed it. During 1952 and 1953 there was a great deal of correspondence with Henry regarding the transfer of the property. He wrote in one letter that he and Alice

> *"had not included in their wills any statements regarding the use of the properties so bequeathed as they did not believe in tying the hands of those receiving the bequests, but it was his wife's and his intent that the property bequeathed should be used for the benefit of the colony which they had established, including the landowners of Bonds Retreat and Cactus Hill."*

Soon after that another structure was proposed by legal counsel. It was recommended that three major organizations be established to manage what

Alice had initiated at Hard Bargain. There would be one for profit and two with tax exempt status:

- The Piscataway Company for the profitable acquisition and sale of real estate in the Moyaone. Its mission was to market land within the Moyaone Reserve.
- The Moyaone Company (a citizen's association) for the operation of recreational projects in the community or colony as it was referred to by Alice and Henry.
- The Alice Ferguson Foundation which would receive the Hard Bargain estate for the operation of educational projects. These educational activities had yet to be identified.

The Alice Ferguson Foundation was officially chartered in autumn of 1954. The charter members were three close friends of Alice who lived in the Moyaone community: Louise North, Mary Thornhill, and Nancy Wagner. They imagined creating a foundation that fostered and supported the local education system. That vision has been realized and more accomplished than perhaps even Alice and Henry could foresee.

The community in Accokeek surrounding Hard Bargain Farm was named "the Moyaone" (pronounced *moy-own*), as a reference to the Indian village on the Potomac that John Smith visited in 1607. This was the same village Alice thought she had discovered when Indian artifacts appeared in the farm's plowed fields near the river shoreline. The Moyaone Reserve as it is now known, is a close-knit community.

The Moyaone had become more settled as word spread about the community through friends of the Fergusons. Indian Head Highway was just two lanes and travel to Accokeek was by country roads. Even though Alice and Henry's neighbors were separated by large tracts of land, they continued to come together on weekends at Hard Bargain for cocktails and play. At these gatherings they "dreamed" the community and envisioned a different lifestyle than that offered by the ever-expanding Washington suburbs.

Henry frequently sought advice from his Moyaone neighbors who jointly decided that to nurture the tender young community, several meeting places providing different functions were needed. Henry had already helped establish a nursery school in the cottage which is next to Bryan Point Road. In 1957 land next to the nursery school was donated by Henry and money set aside for a community recreation area. Playing fields were developed and a swimming pool planned.

Protection of Hard Bargain Farm after Henry's death, and furtherance of educational projects in Southern Maryland were the primary goal of the Alice Ferguson Foundation. Many meetings were held in the 1960s to decide where that mission would lead. The foundation was fumbling around with different ideas. Because there was a teacher shortage, the foundation provided scholarships for teachers. A nature trail across the road from the farm was developed in memory of Max North who served as foundation president 1960-64. In 1966, an agreement was signed with the local school system in Prince George's County to bring school children to the farm for outdoor education. The river, the farm, and the surrounding forests provided the perfect setting for environmental education.

CHAPTER 2

Mount Vernon & the Creation of Piscataway Park

After Alice bought Hard Bargain, she quickly came to realize that the Accokeek community was poor and had no influence with the politicians in Annapolis. As Alice puts it in her book *Adventures in Southern Maryland,* the land was considered "agricultural slums." She thought that, "if she could have just one neighboring gentleman farmer with her point of view then they could get some of the urgent needs in the community like roads cared for." To that end she bought a new farm, Long View, built a house on it and offered it for sale. When she failed to sell Long View, she rented the house and used the farmland as pasture for her cows. Two of the early renters, Charlie Wagner and Robert Straus, were frequent visitors at Hard Bargain and became part of "the gang" as Alice refers to her guests in her memoir.

In the mid-50s the early residents of the Moyaone successfully fended off proposals for housing and commercial developments. These struggles served to create a coalition of people to protect the area. In 1955, residents faced their biggest challenge when a large Texas oil company proposed buying the 500-acre Connelly Farm at the end of Bryan Point Road for an oil storage tank farm. The idea was to bring in oil by the river and then truck it throughout the Washington metro area. The constant flow of large tanker trucks up and down Bryan Point Road, not to mention the danger of oil spills into the river, was a very daunting image. Later there was another serious threat, the construction of a sewer treatment plant at Mockley Point, where Piscataway Creek and the Potomac come together. This was just the tip of the iceberg.

When the oil company proposed purchase of the Connelly Farm, Charlie Wagner and Robert Straus formed an alliance with Cecil Wall, the then resident Director of the Mount Vernon Ladies Association. They learned that Mount Vernon also opposed the construction of an oil tank farm contaminating the Potomac and their riverscape. Alice's husband Henry was involved in many of these conversations and was very protective of the river shore that was his and Alice's former playground and now frequently used by the families in Moyaone.

Those working on preservation of the river shore determined that the solution would be to have it become a national park. This was not a decision arrived at easily. Government protection was cautiously sought and not something one could accomplish overnight. Also, not everyone embraced that solution, including Henry Ferguson. Straus's notes show that Henry, paraphrasing Winston Churchill, actually said "A national park is the worst possible solution except any other." Again, Henry had fond memories of swimming and boating on the river as well as assisting Alice with archeology. I believe his decision came down to a commercial tank farm or a national park.

The Vice Regent of the Mount Vernon Ladies Association at the time was also a congresswoman from Ohio, Representative Frances Bolton. To her credit she fully embraced the protection of the view and believed in the project so fully that she took a bold step. Knowing it would take time, she used her own personal funds to purchase the Connelly farm with the idea of saving it until a national park could be established. On August 10, 1955, Frances Bolton signed a contract for 485 acres. The contract was for $330,000 or $680 an acre. That riverfront land across from Mount Vernon would be worth vastly more today.

Piscataway Park was authorized by Congress in October 1961- a full six years after Frances Bolton purchased the land. It was another seven years and four months before President Kennedy signed the authorization to establish the park. There are approximately 4,700 acres of land preserved to protect the viewshed and two-thirds of that land is privately owned by residents of the Moyaone and protected by scenic easements.

In 1966 my husband Tom and I purchased our five-acre tract and we were present on February 22, 1968, George Washington's birthday, for the dedication of Piscataway Park. Our names are listed on the plaque at the park entrance. We had not yet built our home in the Auburn area of the Reserve, but I remember fondly the day we decided to donate an easement, which limited development on our property to one home and governed how much of our property could be cleared of trees.

Baily Breedlove, the national park ranger in charge of securing the easements, contacted us a few months after our purchase of the land in 1966. He met us at our lot dressed in full uniform including a Smokey the Bear hat. Bailey was a charming fellow well acquainted with the forests edging the river within the park's proposed boundaries. He offered to walk our land with us and pointed out numerous natural and cultural features including the distinctive markings of an old wagon trail that crossed our property and led to Farmington Landing at the end of Farmington Road. We discovered dates carved in an old beech tree dating to 1909, and other signs of what must have been a well-used path to deliver tobacco and other farm goods to the river for further transport. Like many of our neighbors, we simply loved the land and wanted it protected. We agreed to donate an easement not realizing that many others were holding out for an outright purchase.

The Alice Ferguson Foundation was, in the end, a reluctant donor to the creation of the park. The Foundation had signed a cooperative agreement with the Department of the Interior in 1963 agreeing to the donation of 85 acres of riverfront land. A scenic easement was placed on the foundation's remaining private property, and a joint National Park Service/Ferguson Foundation educational program to be conducted on those lands was established.

The land designated to be within the park boundaries is the riverfront portion of Hard Bargain Farm and considered bottomland - the flat fertile land along the river. The record of those events reveals that a new board of directors had been elected and was questioning giving up a valuable asset, 85 acres of riverfront land. The foundation's riverfront land was not easily accessible, as it was bounded by Accokeek Creek and swamp on one side and Piscataway Creek on the other. Unless you arrived by water the only access was across private property. The foundation was finally persuaded on February 14, 1968, to give the last deeds needed to satisfy the criteria for all the lands to bring the park into existence. Henry Ferguson passed away in 1966 so he never saw the national park come into being.

Scenic easements were a new concept, and the five-acre minimum that was originally similar to the covenants that the Moyaone community had set in place were followed. The easements are more enforceable than covenants and come with some tax advantages. The easements donated to the federal government restrict some specific development rights for the sake of preserving the scenic value of the land. They limit industrial and commercial activity; any buildings must be appropriate to homesites and no tree larger than six inches in diameter and 30 feet in height shall be cut down without permission of the National Park Service.

Scenic easements had been used along the Skyline Drive in Virginia, but this area had very little residential occupation. Moyaone was the first community in the United States to use scenic easements as a preservation tool where the land remained on the local tax rolls and residents live with the restrictions that protect the view from Mount Vernon, known as the "Viewshed."

Many actions were involved in the creation of the park, such as additional land purchases, creation and donation of scenic easements, lobbying for funding and seeking tax credits for donors. My neighbors, Robert Straus, Charlie Wagner, George Hanssen, Dixie Otis, Belva Jensen and others used to recount the times they lobbied for the park. Hearing those stories first hand convinced me to do all I could to support the park and the partnerships that were formed to protect the Viewshed.

The author & Le Etta Townsend

CHAPTER 3

I Love Where I Live

I love where I live, and I don't say that lightly but with my whole body, mind, and spirit. When we moved to Accokeek, it was like stepping back in time. Indian Head Highway was only two lanes from Old Fort Road all the way to Indian Head. Our nearest grocery store was six miles away in Fort Washington. Our friends thought we were a bit crazy to move to what was still a very rural area, but early in life I had sought refuge in nature. Because I consider myself an 'earth child', a term that means loving all of nature, Moyaone seemed ideal to me.

My love affair with wild things began in my childhood. There were very few girls in my suburban Norfolk neighborhood. The two girls I knew were older than I and to my disgust preferred playing house, with me being the baby. So, I played alone. When my brother left to play ball with friends, I would have our whole backyard all to myself. It was not a large space, but next-door, our neighbor, Mr. Stallings, must have liked nature too. He made his yard look like a park, mowing the grass and planting a few flowers. In his yard was a stream with a small storybook stone bridge. He allowed my brother and me to play on the bridge and in the stream.

The weather was mild where I lived in Norfolk, so there were lots of plants, animals, and insects in my backyard. We had oak and pecan trees plus many flowers, but the space I liked best was a little rock garden nestled between two very large sweet gum trees. One of the stones behind those trees in the garden was my special seat and it became my hiding place with a nice view of Mr. Stalling's little park.

I remember rejoicing when a bit of that wildlife would show itself to me; little fish in the stream, tadpoles, and an occasional tortoise. Of course, there were many insects but they did not make good playmates. The best was when baby snapping turtles would hatch in the spring. I figured out that you can pick these half dollar sized creatures up by their tails. Their mouths were not big enough to bite so they were harmless. On those spring days when the turtles were there, I would scoop up two or three from the stream and try to make pets of them. I was not allowed to bring them indoors so they became captives outdoors in my mother's shallow pans. It usually took these critters only a day to escape, as it also did with the tadpoles that grew legs and the tortoise that pushed its way out of my barricade.

I also grew to enjoy flowers. During part of my youth, my brother and I had a live-in caretaker named Frieda. She seemed old compared to my parents, and not like other women I knew. Yard work was done on what Frieda called garden days. Those were times when she would don her wide brimmed hat and insist that my brother and I help with weeding and trimming. My brother did not like gardening but I discovered that plants can also be friends. Frieda proclaimed that cloudy damp days were the best time to garden because we wouldn't get sunburned or too hot.

When plants are cared for properly, we were rewarded with fragrant displays of beautiful flowers. Frieda was from England and somehow knew how to make our yard beautiful, so much so that the garden club often gave us ribbons. Doing yard work didn't seem like work to me. It was fun. Frieda would tell me about each plant including the weeds and explained things about the soil, like why earthworms were like gold. Frieda explained that worms eat leaves and other organic matter so that plants can use it. Their castings make the soil fertile. I know her love for me and the garden helped root me to the earth.

We lived very near the Chesapeake Bay, and on hot summer nights fans offered very little relief from the heat and humidity. Our family could drive to the bay in only 20 minutes. Several evenings a week during those hot spells we would go to the public beach for a swim in the bay. Because I fished, swam, and played in these incredible places I learned to love the wildlife.

When I married, I left Norfolk but still yearned for nature. Luckily, my husband had grown up on a lake and had a similar passion. The early years of our marriage were filled with change. I finished my last year of college in 1965, majoring in sociology. Tom, an engineer, accepted a position in the Washington, D.C. area. We moved and bought a home in Oxon Hill, Maryland, and shortly afterward we started a family. While attending a meeting of the League of Women Voters in Oxon Hill, I learned about the Moyaone community from Eloise Swick and Frances Wright who were early residents of the Moyaone Reserve. They told me that Alice Ferguson had bought up land surrounding Hard Bargain in the 1940s and then sold it to friends and friends of friends. They said the lots were a minimum of five acres and that land was still for sale.

I was curious about this place as Tom and I wanted a country home where we could raise our family. One Sunday in July 1966, we visited the Piscataway Company, a small real estate enterprise staffed by local residents of the Moyaone community. I'll never forget that first introduction to the Moyaone. It was a hot July day and I was expecting our first child when I traipsed over several pieces of land. The area was beautiful, the people we met were lovely, and we put a contract on a lot almost immediately after that first trip to Accokeek. In 1968, we built a little home at the far bottom of a winding road. I had a two-year-old son, Leo and a six-month-old daughter, Laura at the time. In 1970, I gave birth to a third child, Roger our second son.

After settling in on our lot in the Moyaone we discovered all kinds of wildlife and in the spring, carpets of wildflowers only steps from our back door. We also have fox, deer, and many species of birds. Twenty wild turkeys in our yard is not an unusual occurrence. For me, Accokeek and the Moyaone is 'earth child heaven'. The neighbors I met in church and child play groups in the community were of similar background to mine, enjoying the freedom to develop their little homesteads as they chose.

Along with the excitement of raising a family, building a home, and moving to Accokeek, two years into my marriage my parents died. Their separate passings in 1967 and 1969 came between the births of my three children. In three-and-a-half years I gave birth to three children, lost both parents and built and moved to a new home. It was hard for me. I coped with the sadness and change by immersing myself into raising toddlers, gardening, joining a neighborhood play group and continuing a part-time job as a leader of University of Maryland-sponsored parent discussion groups. By 1975, things had settled down a bit. My neighbors had become good friends, and I was also involved in community activities. With my three children all in school for full or partial days, I began to feel restless – I needed something more to do.

Pat Vanderslice, my nearest neighbor, told me about a need for educators at the nearby Alice Ferguson Foundation's Hard Bargain Farm. This was in 1975 and the foundation's board and the executive director had established an outdoor education program at the farm. The job entailed leading elementary school children around the farm and on nature trails. At that time kindergarten through third graders came for day-long field trips and a special overnight program that served fifth graders. Pat was going to pursue this opportunity herself and I decided to apply as well. We both won jobs and shortly afterward were sworn in as national park rangers. In those years all the educators hired for naturalist positions at the foundation were paid by the National Park Service as part of a cooperative agreement to establish the park. As part-timers we didn't wear uniforms but were allowed to participate in National Park Service training. This endeavor was the beginning of my career at the farm.

CHAPTER 4

My Introduction to Hard Bargain Farm

TEACHING ABOUT THE ENVIRONMENT on an operating farm to school children opened a whole new world for me. Working alongside others who loved nature helped me identify my life's purpose. Though I didn't have any idea as to how this would play out, it fulfilled a desire to share my love of nature. It was the perfect job for me, allowing me to lead the school children through the farm between the hours of 10:00 a.m. and 2:00 p.m. and then be home to greet my own three youngsters, ages 5, 7, and 9.

I had learned in my youth that people like my caretaker Frieda are our real teachers and can nurture the love of plants and animals in all of us. Also, there's a great need to protect and preserve parks, forests, rivers and lakes, where we can be free to explore the natural environment. My passion for wild things was instrumental in guiding the programs that the staff created at Hard Bargain. It never seemed like work to me because my heart was and still is with the child in me that treasures the earth. It's something I want for children everywhere, and have worked to achieve that goal.

Though I had very little knowledge of farming, I learned from co-workers and from our resident farmer Hank Xander. Lunch with Hank and the staff was often a highlight of the day, with eight of us sitting around the rickety picnic table telling tales and teaching each other by example. We came from different backgrounds, and many were former teachers. It was during these times of sharing that I learned to bake yeast bread, how to make wonderful soups, and plucked chickens (and cooked one!). I also took a woodworking course and used wood from the farm to make furniture. I steeped myself in the ways of the farm much like women in farm communities have done for decades.

Evelyn Biles

One staff member I particularly enjoyed was Evelyn Biles. She was the most senior person on staff and had been a teacher at the nursery school formed by Henry Ferguson for neighborhood children. Evelyn reminded me of a very wise grandmother who delights little children by her uncanny ability to see with a child's eyes. She did things like gather a hen from the chicken coop as she told the story of Henny Penny, and made a fuss over animal poop in the barnyard which sent the kids into peals of laughter.

One day Evelyn reported that a six-foot-long black snake that lived in the cabin on the hill was draped over the large bush outside the window. We knew that on sunny days a snake came out and took a sunbath in the bush. She turned the sighting into a safari of great importance. Following the same trails and sharing stories, we learned that animals have routines that are and were predictable. There was nothing to fear, it was just something that was repeated time and again. I learned from Evelyn and others to be watchful and to appreciate these gifts of nature. After a period of time, nature trails and the farm buildings revealed things to us that a casual visitor overlooks; swallows in the barn rafters, cave crickets in the root cellar, and mice in the corn crib. The cycle of life on the farm and sharing it daily with co-workers and visitors was a joy-filled time for me.

This incidental learning was strengthened by courses and field trips we took in the summer. One neighbor family, the Jensen's, were very involved in the early years in the creation of the farm's environmental program. Roy and Belva Jensen settled in the Moyaone in 1959. They were biology teachers at Gwynn Park High School. In 1965 Roy became the first director of outdoor education at Hard Bargain and built the Max North Nature Trail in memory of one of the Alice Ferguson Foundation's first presidents. Belva became the head of the biology department at Charles County Community College and it was through her efforts that the education staff at the foundation received more formal training in summer teacher workshops.

Eileen Watts, another staff member, was my first tutor in the ways of the farm and an excellent naturalist. One day she told us that 30 baby chicks had arrived at the post office and she asked if anyone wanted to go with her after work to fetch them. I offered to help. We took the rather dilapidated farm truck to the post office. When we entered, the room reverberated with loud cheeping sounds of what seemed like hundreds of baby chicks. But when handed over by the post mistress, it was only a single package of 30 pullets (baby laying hens). They came all snuggled together in a shallow flat box with vent holes. I got to hold the precious package on my lap as we drove back to the farm.

I then helped introduce them to their new home, the brooder house, located near the farmer's cottage where they were warmed by a special light. From the beginning Eileen took on these kinds of chores as a way of assisting our farmer. Shortly afterwards Eileen became the caretaker for the farm's newly purchased dairy cow Favor. It delighted me, a country girl at heart, learning to master farm life.

CHAPTER 5

My First Boss

HARD BARGAIN CAPTURED MY HEART and the hearts of the dedicated staff working there. Bernie Wareham, the very first executive director of the foundation, and my first boss taught me the ways of Hard Bargain Farm, a place that he nurtured and loved. I still feel that same deep connection. I also agree with Wendell Berry, poet, essayist, novelist, farmer and conservationist, states in his writings on rural farm communities that,

> *"those who settle and love the life they have made and the place they have made it into develop a great affection for the land."*

Berry further believes that the countryside is in serious decline because of the reduced number of small farm communities. For any place to survive, there needs to be people watching - the way a farmer comes to know his soil type, weather patterns, crop production, and more. If there aren't enough people watching day by day then serious changes take place. And nobody noticies.

Bernie Wareham was a watcher and he showed in his actions a great affection for Hard Bargain and the Moyaone Community. In Alice's writings I see that same thread of devotion to Hard Bargain and to the friends she attracted to Accokeek. That devotion was an underpinning of the Foundation's education program when I began working there.

When Henry died in 1966 there were no Fergusons left to care for the Farm. The founders of the newly created foundation envisioned that Hard Bargain would be a great location to teach about farm life and nature. Those founders' love for Hard Bargain was anchored in their associations with Henry and Alice. Bernie's job as the first full-time paid executive was to get the newly-established farm education program that hosted school children on field trips on solid footing. Bernie wore many hats as the overseer of the then 20 year old organization that had been established in 1954. In his demanding position he was at once administrator, educator, farm hand, custodian, teacher, and boss. Bernie lived close by in the Moyaone and had known Henry Ferguson.

I began working as a park ranger/naturalist in 1975. And, in those days, Bernie helped me learn about trees, farm animals, the river, and how to share nature's magic with children. Bernie always arrived on the scene in a little red jeep. He would frequently roll up to the overnight lodge with provisions for the children's dinner (at that time catered out of a local school) and often with tasks for staff to tackle when they were not with students. His philosophy demanded that he and everyone associated with the farm be on the go. He hung a sign in the lodge that was an old Chinese proverb: *"I hear and I forget, I see and I remember, I do and I understand."*

I don't know when Bernie did his office work because if you were shepherding children on any day around this 350-acre farm you could count on seeing the red jeep and Bernie. At first, I was nervous when the jeep approached because I wanted to please him. His standards were very high. You knew right away if something was amiss because Bernie's ever-present smile would disappear and with a stern visage the misdeed (such as trash not emptied) was corrected. He wanted all of us to buy into his vision of teaching children to know where their food was grown and how to care for the earth. With this as a driving force in his life, he and his trusty red jeep tirelessly delivered goods, hauled hay, stuffed mail boxes with annual reports, and tracked down his charges. When the red jeep showed up, we better not be sitting!

As I got to know Bernie, I discovered that he had grown up on a farm in Ohio. Later he was a school teacher and then a principal, but eventually ended up working in research and development for the Naval Research Lab and the Department of Defense. After leaving his government job he was hired as the Alice Ferguson Foundation executive director.

Daily he worked to foster the newly-instituted environmental education program conducted in partnership with the Prince George's County and Charles County School Systems. In the beginning, classes of students would come on day visits to the farm and hike on a nature trail. Later fifth grade students would spend a night, with the boys sleeping in the barn and the girls sleeping in the cottage located near the Moyaone pool. Because of the potential fire hazard and lack of bathrooms the health department vetoed this arrangement. At that time there was an outhouse in the barnyard. An emergency step was taken to have the boys and girls share a divided bunk space separated by a partition in the Moyaone Community building, generously leased to the foundation for one dollar a year plus utilities. One of Bernie's great accomplishments was to design and supervise the building of an overnight lodge in 1976. Later the building was dedicated to him and called Wareham Lodge. It served students with very modest accommodations until 2017 when new sleeping quarters were built.

The Alice Ferguson Foundation was governed by a seven-member all-volunteer board, most of them residents of the Moyaone Reserve. During the work week, it was Bernie who was in the driver's seat, as he set the tone for the fledgling environmental education program. Bernie expected us to teach the children through example. Our farm walks meant gathering eggs from under the chickens, slopping the hogs with leftover scraps from lunch and dinner, and letting these city children climb and jump in the hay loft. If hay had been baled, we assisted the fifth-grade kids as they loaded it into the barn. Bernie didn't care if the bales were too heavy. He was old-school and nothing was beyond the limits of students, teachers, and staff.

Some of Bernie's ideas and methods still linger with me. I can hear him now, "Give the trouble makers a job to do, like opening and closing gates. Make sure you show the children how to mop the floor before the class departs. If there is trash anywhere, have the children pick it up and dispose of it." He showed us through example how to carry out these chores.

Every new staff member was required to follow Bernie on a tour of the farm. I remember the day I followed him. We started out from the lodge with about ten students, all of them following behind; a rule that was firmly enforced. Suddenly he stopped in the middle of the grassy field and asked if anyone knew where we were standing or what it was called. These city children looked puzzled and he gave a clue by pointing to a small pile of manure. "What animal has been here?" he asked. The puzzle was solved as they learned about pastures. But we could not leave the spot because something was there that didn't belong. Again, the children pondered until one child spotted a gum wrapper. Bernie pointed out that we don't leave trash around the farm. It just isn't a good practice to litter the earth with trash. The boy was instructed to pick the paper up until we found a trash can and the rest of the class was deputized as guardians of the land and to watch for litter. Bernie was a master of getting the children involved and thinking about this place unknown to them before their field trip. No one resented these declarations because experience taught that they worked. Bernie's upbeat attitude infected us all and we learned by doing. Many of us volunteered to do farm chores beyond our scheduled shift. It was one way that Hard Bargain got into my blood. I loved the job, the farm, and the staff.

Little by little I became acquainted with some of the early residents and charter members of the foundation. Nancy Wagner, Elizabeth Kenah, Louise North and others were working behind the scenes to keep Hard Bargain as Alice intended it, "a place for good times". These pioneers had figured that by creating the education program they could serve the local community school systems and keep Alice's and Henry's spirit alive. Meanwhile, building the lodge, and a stock market downturn had reduced the foundation's endowment by almost 30 per cent. One day at a staff meeting Bernie asked if anyone had experience writing grants. Though I knew nothing of grant writing, I volunteered to give it a try. The grant was being given by the Institute of Museum Services and our foundation qualified because living history farms are considered museums. I learned how much money it took to operate the foundation and its program. The foundation didn't get the grant, but I learned a lot of new things about this intriguing nonprofit. Grant writing became a big puzzle that I wanted to solve.

In 1979, Bernie was in his early 70s and had announced his retirement. We all wondered who would replace him. Later that spring, Bernie surprised me when he called me aside and asked if I would like to apply for his job. He wanted someone who was dedicated to the program. I was one of the youngest staff members and definitely had enthusiasm for the foundation's programs. So, it was a no-brainer for me. I went home, talked with my husband and began working on my resume. In July 1979 I began my new job. As I was making my first budget, I discovered another fact about Bernie - for several years, he had not been taking his $10,000 annual salary, yet he was still giving with all his heart. Bernie died in 2003, just shy of his 95th birthday. He lived fully in those 15 years of retirement from the Foundation, with the same energy of a much younger person. He stayed away from the office but would come by in the same little red jeep to help bale hay, mow pastures or work the membership table at festivals.

When people ask me about how I came to be employed at Hard Bargain, I usually tell them that like Bernie I also drove a red 4x4, but my vehicle was a Land Rover. And then I'd add that Bernie Wareham created some amazing tracks that I wanted to follow.

CHAPTER 6

Becoming the Director

I've always felt that it was somewhat remarkable that I was chosen to succeed Bernie Wareham as executive director of the foundation. In today's world with jobs like this being highly competitive, it might be considered a miracle. I have spent a lot of time thinking about the confluence of events that put me in this wonderful job. I'm sure I had an edge because there were very few applicants and I was the only one that lived in the Moyaone. I was filled with enthusiasm, had tried my hand at grant writing, and was eager to implement some ideas for promoting the farm and its programs. Something I thought the search committee overlooked was that I had very limited office experience.

On my first day as the executive director of the Alice Ferguson Foundation, I remember feeling a bit overwhelmed. My job as a park ranger/naturalist turned out to be an apprenticeship. It had led me to appreciate all resources that the Alice Ferguson Foundation had to offer.

I was one of three full-time employees: myself, the farm manager, and a secretary. Another part-time person helped with the farm. The foundation's payroll was more than 70 percent of its $90,000 budget. The education staff was paid by the National Park Service. At that time there were about seven women working as part-time park rangers and each earned about $2,500 per year.

I really looked forward to managing the foundation. In the past I had been limited by the daily routines of sharing the place with classes of students. Now I had the freedom to examine every aspect of the farm and its surrounds without being questioned. With this new position my curiosity took over. I had spent several years in the educational program learning everything I could about Hard Bargain. This new venture unleashed my explorer self and I was definitely in uncharted waters.

I was honestly naive about my management role. Every facet of the position demanded that I be open to suggestions. When trying my hand at raising money, hosting special events, recruiting volunteers, program development, marketing, budgeting, attending endowment management meetings, hiring staff and working with politicians, being curious and open was my modus operandi. Today most private nonprofits have separate positions for those tasks. I had to learn and do the best I could with all of it. I came to the job realizing that it would stretch me; little did I realize how much I would need to learn. Luckily two of my favorite activities in college were helpful. The first was being the only woman on the Old Dominion University's debate team and the second was a work study job in the research department of the library. I had learned how to find things out and then organize and sell an argument.

One of my first actions was to ask neighbors and friends what they thought the job of the executive director should focus on. I had a one-page position description but it contained very basic responsibilities like making sure the bills were paid and maintaining school group schedules. I got lots of good advice. Several neighbors who knew something about the stock market recommended more oversight of the endowment managers. At my recommendation the board of directors established a finance committee. That group included my husband Tom who is a CPA, Joseph DeStefanis who specialized in tax law, Cy Adams, our bookkeeper, and Elmer Biles, a board member and statistician. They became a trusted finance committee that met quarterly with the advisors. My husband Tom helped me put together a realistic budget and the endowment began to grow. In 1979 the endowment was valued at less than one million dollars. When I retired in 1999, with better oversight, fundraising, and careful budgeting it had grown to more than five million dollars.

The most memorable of all that advice was from a neighbor, Scott Odell, who at that time was a curator/administrator at the Smithsonian Museum of American History. He said, "Kay, you have been given a turn-of-the-century family farm, carefully planned by Alice Ferguson. Someday the park service or another group will want to spend millions of dollars to create one. You have one so don't lose it." He saw the importance of small farms in our history and the importance of demonstrating how they have fed our nation.

I want to clarify here that there are two operating farms run by two separate foundations in Accokeek. It was common that new residents and visitors just coming to experience one of these farms would be confused. I could see that one of my responsibilities was to make Hard Bargain Farm stand out as a leader in environmental education and still preserve the lovely small farm Alice had created.

The National Colonial Farm, located at the end of Bryan Point road and operated by the Accokeek Foundation, is totally located within the boundaries of Piscataway Park, governed by a board of directors which must follow the guidelines set out in use permits granted through the National Park Service. This farm's mission was sharing the colonial heritage that existed in George Washington's day, with demonstrations of spinning wool and cooking in the outdoor kitchen. The Accokeek Foundation's other purpose was to preserve the view from Mount Vernon, an effort led by its first president, founder and park champion, Robert Ware Straus. The Accokeek Foundation was instrumental in getting Piscataway Park established and has very close ties to the Mount Vernon Ladies Association and the National Park Service. The Colonial farm is open daily to the public and it hosts many school fieldtrips.

The Alice Ferguson Foundation was organized for more general educational purposes that included farm tours of Hard Bargain and ecology taught on the nature trails. The foundation was serving school children from Charles and Prince George's County a cooperative effort where teachers from the visiting schools even taught some of the classes. It's more like a school and not open to the public.

The Alice Ferguson Foundation was just establishing itself and was following a path that was similar to many other small family foundations. The organization was started in Alice's memory and staffed largely by volunteers who brainstormed many ideas concerning its primary purpose. While Henry Ferguson was alive and still in residence at Hard Bargain, those early ventures were teacher scholarships to stem the teacher shortage, and a nursery school for local children in the farm's cottage.

When I was hired as executive director, the identity of the foundation was still forming. The park rangers at the foundation were teaching several thousand students a year the foundation's mission of "how we manage our land to produce food." Pulling together the lovely small family farm with a nature component was the beginning of an environmental program. I could envision a larger role for the foundation which would require more paid staff and outreach to the general public. It was going to be a challenge I enjoyed. However, those plans were put on hold!

CHAPTER 7

Legislation Brings Conflict & a New Path

When Alice decided to unearth the American Indian artifacts and burials located on the Potomac River shore at Hard Bargain, I doubt she would ever have imagined the outcome. From her writings I know it was a heartfelt commitment meant to enhance our understanding of the native cultures, preserve the remnants of the Piscataway's life on the river, and to publish her findings. In the 30s all archeological study was taking place in the west, so institutions conducting research were not interested in her project.

Ultimately, her work which ended up being a collaborative effort with the Smithsonian brought attention to the native cultures that inhabited Accokeek. Alice's research, and that done by others, has revealed that the Piscataways were the primary tribal group inhabiting the Potomac shore. The Indian Removal Act of 1830 required Native Americans to move elsewhere. As a result, small groups from tribal villages did their best to avoid being relocated to the west and moved into the Zekiah Swamp. They remain in Southern Maryland and have worked hard to trace their relationships to the Piscataway Tribe. Alice's published work has been celebrated and studied by many and the archeological site, so carefully explored, became a National Historic Landmark known at the Accokeek Creek Site.

On August 5, 1979, there was a headline in the Washington Post that read, *"Congress votes to bury Chief Turkey Tayac in Piscataway Park".* I was only one month into my new job and this legislation had a profound effect on my first few years leading the foundation. The location of the proposed burial site was to be at the Accokeek Creek Site which was bounded by the river, a marsh and the foundation's private property. The only access was on the foundation's gravel road which passed only 20 feet from the overnight lodge and through the pasture where our cows often grazed. This put the foundation at odds with the National Park Service and the special use conveyed to the foundation with the donation of the land, because it could imply an easement on Hard Bargain's private road and allow for unlimited public access. Turkey Tayac had helped Alice with her archeological investigations. His birth name was Phillip Sheraton Proctor but he referred to himself as Chief Turkey. He was doing his best to preserve his native culture.

I met him only one time when my husband and I attended a neighbor's party in the summer of 1976 where he was a featured guest. He was introduced to us as Turkey, a person of American Indian heritage who had helped Alice to excavate the burial grounds down by the river. Turkey was a small, elderly, ruddy-complexioned man dressed in khaki clothing and he had with him an elaborate Indian headdress. I guessed that Turkey was in his mid-70s. He sat in the corner of this crowded room, surrounded by people who were mesmerized by his stories. My husband was one of them and recounted later Turkey's discussion of herbal medicine.

Before Chief Turkey's death he made a request to the National Park Service to be buried in Piscataway Park. Turkey had told the Park Service and our congressional representatives that Alice gave 20 acres of the land to him, but that the deed was never recorded. Also, he claimed that he had donated this parcel to establish the national park. In time it became clear that neither the National Park Service nor the staff of the congressman who had sponsored the legislation checked the public land records. Congressman Philip Burton of California was a powerful member of the House appropriations committee.

The sudden death of Congressman Goodlow Byron of Maryland, a champion of national parks, provided a way for Chief Turkey's burial in Accokeek. Legislation allowing Congressman Byron's burial in Antietam National Cemetery reversed a federal policy forbidding burials in national parks. The pending legislation regarding Turkey Tayac's burial was added as a rider to the Goodlow Byron Act and unfortunately implied that the government had an easement on the foundation's private road. The impending burial of Turkey Tayac required that the foundation take drastic action to defend itself against an implied easement for the public and continued trespass on its private property. The Tayac family, the National Park Service, and Congressman Burton were not pleased when the foundation denied access for the interment of Chief Turkey. We couldn't allow the legislation to threaten use of our private land.

In the Congressional Record on October 9, 1979, the claim that Turkey Tayac had donated the land was corrected when Congressman Phillip Burton stated:

> *"I would like to further note that the passage of this legislation should not and cannot in anyway lead to the conclusion that we have determined that the Piscataways have granted or ceded these properties to the National Park Service. It is my clear view that it is in fact the Alice Ferguson Foundation that granted the properties under discussion to the National Park Service. This legislation cannot be construed and should not be construed in any way to diminish the current special use permit privileges exercised by the Alice Ferguson Foundation."*

Even this reassurance didn't stop the pressure to allow unlimited access through the farm. On the day of Turkey's burial, the foundation allowed a walking procession over its road with a shuttle for the handicapped. Chief Tayac was interred on November 12, 1979, and his son Billy was anointed chief. For the next six years the only way to get to that area was across Hard Bargain's private road. The Tayac family had asked for 24-hour access over the farm road and received lots of press coverage, always putting the foundation on the defensive.

The claims made by Chief Turkey, his son Billy, and his followers required constant vigilance by the foundation and considerable effort to correct the record. In one media appearance associated with a special ceremony, Chief Turkey's grandson, Mark Tayac, threatened to tear down the foundation's farm gate. The Maryland State Police guarded our property that day. Occasionally strangers wanting to go to the burial site would knock on the door of the overnight lodge asking to use the restroom. It was frightening for the teachers and chaperones who were there with their students. The constant pressure led us to the decision to put locks on our gates. Today even the notion of unauthorized access to educational facilities would bring about lockdowns in a school.

Fortunately, this battle was not fought with bows, arrows, and guns. It took place on paper, with letters to Congress, public demonstrations, legal opinions, numerous meetings, and news reports. The Piscataway Indian Nation, Inc. felt that their First Amendment rights were violated because this was sacred land- the equivalent of their church - and they were being denied access. The foundation's position was supported by legal precedent that the government couldn't declare it public domain because it would violate the Establishment Clause of the Constitution by aiding a religion. The foundation lawyers found constitutional support for the foundation's position. There was no easement granted when the land was conveyed to establish the park and so the National Park Service couldn't force us to provide access. It concluded that National Park staff had access to the site for maintenance and patrol, but couldn't convey access to the public. In the meantime, the foundation learned that other tribal groups in the area also wanted access because it was not just the burial site of Chief Turkey but also the ossuaries of their ancestors. Despite the conflict over use of the road we sympathized with those who wanted to get to the burial area. The foundation continued to ask the park service to develop an alternative access.

Bill Moran, at that time chairman of the Moyaone Public Affairs Committee, helped us brainstorm a solution to the problem. What if the approach to the Tayac burial site was one that fostered an appreciation for the environment and the culture of the native people? The land surrounding the burial site was bounded by river, marsh and swampland. The topography made it impossible to build an alternative road. We brainstormed several ideas and decided that a nature trail would suffice.

My husband Tom and another neighbor, Bill Gallagher, both engineers, took on the task to find another way to access the area. What they proposed was a boardwalk entry from the opposite side of the marsh with vehicular access through the parkland to a parking area. The boardwalk would be an extensive building project as it would be approximately a half mile in length, but it was doable. Bill drew up the plan and mapped it out. The foundation board members presented it to the National Park Service Regional Director Jack Fish.

In the meantime, the National Park Service allowed me to attend a conference on Native American sacred sites and practices at the Grand Canyon. It was led by a national park ranger who was in fact a Native American. At the conference I learned that land considered sacred to native peoples is often in remote places and not accessible to the general public. This ensures their culture being honored by those who visit.

After about a year of meetings and surveys by park planners, ecologists and archeologists, our plan was presented for public hearings. There was concern in the neighborhood about unwanted elements like litter and crime that would be attracted to the area. But on the whole, it was judged a good solution. The boardwalk was constructed and opened in 1985. The foundation when notified in advance continues to provide limited access to a few vehicles over its private property to a few vehicles.

The boardwalk stretches across the marsh at the mouth of Accokeek Creek as it joins the Potomac. The half mile walk is beautiful in the fall with the marsh grasses turning a golden yellow giving forth to views of Mount Vernon just across the river. It was a win/win for all. The Piscataway and the general public have a lovely trail to reach the riverfront and the Turkey Tayac burial site. The foundation gained a beautiful study area for the school children to learn about the environment.

CHAPTER 8

Alice's Home Becomes Foundation Headquarters

When I began my job as the foundation's executive director, I embraced the place with great enthusiasm. However, I knew to be cautious because I was inexperienced as an administrator and I was aware that routines had been establish over the last 10 years. I wanted to benefit from those routines but also to find my own style.

My predecessor, 70-year old Bernie Wareham, retired because he had concluded there were too many senior citizens running the place. One of those seniors was my very first secretary, Mrs. Wilhelmina Xander. Mrs. Xander, the wife of Alice Ferguson's farm manager, spent most of her adult life at the farm and raised four children there. Her youngest, Henry Xander Jr. (nicknamed Hank), became the farm manager the first year I was director. Beginning with Alice's hiring of Henry Sr. and extending through to Hank's retirement, one or more Xanders have lived and taken care of Hard Bargain for more than 80 years!

Following Henry Ferguson's death, the foundation's board decided that the farmhouse shouldn't sit empty, so Mrs. Xander was asked to live there during the week and to serve in the capacity of hostess and secretary. As hostess she welcomed groups for meetings, and she assisted Bernie Wareham with office duties. Even though she looked fragile and petite, Mrs. Xander was a sturdy woman.

I discovered that as the foundation's secretary, rather than use the office she preferred to stand guard over the office phone by using the extension in the farmhouse's bright yellow kitchen. She spent most days seated there on an antique wooden chair that was made more comfortable by using a cushion. This was the only such chair in the house and we all knew it to be Mrs. Xander's seat. Other chairs in the kitchen were white enameled that matched the table and were from the Ferguson years at the farm – these were ours to use.

Seated in her favorite chair and dressed in her favorite office attire (a print house dress) Mrs. Xander was quite equal to the chores of our antiquated system. In those days there were no computers, copiers, fax machines, or intercoms. Mrs. Xander used her trusty shorthand, acquired in earlier jobs at the Indian Head Naval Base, to record messages on recycled IBM punch cards. This was her equivalent to the sticky notes we use today. Being thrifty, she used the old punch cards for everything: messages, memos, and recipes. Messages were transferred to a spiral notebook in the office and I still have a few punch cards in my recipe file at home.

From her post in the kitchen Mrs. Xander would also cook up delicious food. The fragrance of soups, stews, and yeast rolls often wafted throughout the house. It was a pleasant and comfortable routine, perfectly suited to her - and also to me.

Mrs. Xander and I used the same office. It had been the room that Alice had set up as a guest bedroom off the side porch. Mrs. Xander typed the foundation's business letters, making carbon-paper copies for the file. She also typed the dreaded stencils for mimeographed annual reports to members. I believe I made her nervous because I soon discovered that she preferred to do her typing when I was not in the office. Each morning when I arrived if I thought she needed time to finish typing a letter or stencil, I would make an excuse to disappear to some other part of the farm.

In my second year, the foundation board approved hiring another part-time secretary. I chose a neighbor, Le Etta Townsend, and gave her the title of administrative assistant so that Mrs. Xander would not think she had been replaced. Le Etta worked three mornings a week. She and I planned in detail how the three of us could work in the same office. Le Etta's desk was the smallest with a little fold out work area. She relieved Mrs. Xander of scheduling school groups, typing letters, and communicating with the education staff.

Because we were all crowded in the front office it wasn't long before Le Etta and I conspired to turn the second guest bedroom on the ground floor into an office for me. The rest of the house looked just like it did when Alice and Henry lived there.

Le Etta proved to be the perfect person I needed to help move things forward. I could visualize improving the education program, attracting more community participation, and creating publications. With her help I was able to more clearly visualize my hopes and plans for the foundation and focus on priorities. Le Etta became a key person in the expansion of the foundation and the smooth function of the office. She stayed long after I retired, serving as office manager to a much larger staff.

The foundation was so integrated in the Moyaone community that all news of the foundation's activities was reported on the last page of *Smoke Signals*, the community newsletter. Our staff brainstormed the idea of a separate publication and its production, and Moyaone resident Gordon Watts designed a masthead for the proposed newsletter. Gordon enthusiastically set to work creating publications and tickets for special events on the antique printing press set up in his basement. On approval, the new publication, *Hard Bargain News*, debuted in October 1980 and served to significantly broaden the membership's view of the foundation including news of its educational activities.

Our first few years were busy and productive. We created an independent newsletter, a new brochure, and we graduated beyond mimeographed annual reports to more polished publications. Additionally, our staff established the Spring Farm Festival, and the Oktoberfest, and with outside help we renovated much of the farmhouse. Le Etta helped me keep those projects on track.

Certain routines had been established before I was hired. One was the Friday visit by our bookkeeper, Major Cy Adams. He would come in on Friday afternoons to pay bills, do the payroll, and create financial reports - all with a tedious double entry bookkeeping system. Major Adams lived in the Moyaone on Bryan Point Road. He was another early resident and nearing 70. A retired army major, he was a very precise person and often arrived in a sports car and decked out in a beautiful tweed jacket with ascot. He told us much about his varied careers and travels all over Europe. He had wonderful stories about the foundation and his associations with the neighborhood. Those insights were valuable to us. The long-established routines and dedicated volunteers were important to our understanding of the early workings of the foundation.

As Le Etta became a fulltime employee, she, like everyone on the staff, led farm tours and kept me in touch with the goings-on of our part-time educational staff. My desk would be stacked with correspondence to answer, partially written grants, draft budgets, and lists of volunteers to contact for the next special event. I would be overwhelmed with office work and forget what was important. Le Etta managed to gently remind me every day of the next thing to do or next phone call to make. She was indispensable to me.

About a year after Le Etta joined the staff, Mrs. Xander became ill. There were pains in her chest and she had not seen a doctor since her children were born. She would not leave her bed in her small upstairs bedroom and was convinced she was dying. I took matters into my own hands and called a close friend and nurse, Beth Nicholson. Mrs. Xander knew Beth and consented to a house call. Beth took her blood pressure and talked her into seeing a doctor. It was discovered that she was having angina attacks. She quickly got over her fear of doctors and proudly wore a little container of nitro pills around her neck. Mrs. Xander had another home nearby, so soon after this episode her family convinced her to move there permanently. As the organization grew, we learned to be more efficient, but Mrs. Xander's presence had firmly set in place a relaxed tone that foundation employees appreciated for many years.

The early days were challenging and budgets were tight. By the early 80s we were able to purchase a computer and a copy machine. No more driving the two miles up to the highway to copy important documents at five cents apiece.

From the start I was in love with the farmhouse where I spent a lot of my time. My office was in a downstairs bedroom in the guest wing. My desk was placed next to a window and I had a view of the river. Often our education staff would bring children up to that window and wave to me. The living room was furnished just as Alice and Henry left it, with lovely upholstered furniture, the grand piano, and Alice's paintings which celebrate the many good times she and Henry shared at the farm.

I especially loved the large country kitchen. It is so big that when I first stepped into the bright yellow space with white painted cabinets, I immediately imagined all kinds of harvesting and canning projects. At this time there were no great preserving chores being conducted, but when I arrived, evidence of that past could be found in the canning cellar where ancient jars of green beans and tomatoes were still stored on dusty shelves. Later, those items were destroyed so that no one would decide they were safe to eat. I was in favor of leaving them, but lost to the cause of safety.

The two large casement windows that open out onto the narrow-screened side porch made the kitchen seem even larger. We used the porch to store goods for special events and to deposit boots and coats in foul weather. In summer, when the windows were open, the kitchen would take on an airy feel, letting the fragrances of the flower and herb gardens fill the room.

Our staff felt privileged to use Alice's collection of dishes as everyday ware which connected us to her in a special way. I was especially fond of the plates that were hand painted with elaborate and colorful designs. Using them made me feel like I was time traveling back to those days when Alice was serving as hostess to friends on weekends. I believe these dishes are now tucked away in a safe place and used only for special guests.

In the early 80s our small staff would sit around the white enameled table. As the staff grew so did the crowd around the table. Around noon someone would announce that the tea kettle had been put on. That meant we would all be gathering in 10 minutes for lunch. This is where we often 'cooked up' the next educational program, brainstormed ideas for special events, or just made playful conversation.

One spring day in the early 90s, we were bemoaning the fact that the vegetable garden was filled with chick weed. We had established a garden just off the kitchen on the very spot where Alice had a victory garden during the war. Many of us had fenced plots there. I wondered out loud why it was called chick weed which spurned the idea that perhaps the chickens favored it and perhaps if we brought several chickens up to the garden, they would do our weeding for us. So immediately after lunch three of us went down to the chicken coop and gathered up three hens. We deposited them in the fenced garden and waited to see if our plan would work. As we watched, the chickens just wandered around so we went back to our work hopeful that the garden would be weeded by the end of the day. The results were not positive. After four hours in the garden the chickens had spent all their time digging and eating worms from the compost pile. Later that week we all got down to the chore of weeding!

One thing I enjoyed most was just sitting in the kitchen lingering over a cup of coffee or tea and sharing farm tales with a staff who were more like friends. Sometimes without notice a gentle breeze would blow just enough so that the back door would fall open. This happened so many times that we came to imagine that Alice was joining us. Occasionally someone would say, "There's Alice again" - I hoped it was true and that she shared some of our good times in the kitchen, which were often the best part of the day.

Hank Xander

CHAPTER 9

The Working Farm

Hard Bargain was always more than a place of work to those of us who were charged with the responsibility of keeping things functioning. The farmhouse, outbuildings, cabin, fields, and pastures represented a period of history that was disappearing. Alice's friends, the early residents that we had come to know, impressed on us the importance of protecting the place she had created.

I was fortunate in that Hank Xander, Eileen Watts, and I immediately became a team. The day-to-day running of the farm, education program, and administration of the foundation was in our laps. I remember that soon after I was hired, I met with Hank and Eileen to talk about what it would be like when Bernie left and how we could support each other. Hank, Eileen, and I were the only full-time employees and there was a lot to do.

I know that each of us grasped the importance of Hard Bargain and its history. The farm was a place that had united the Moyaone community and the three of us lived in the community. It was also serving as a model for agricultural and environmental education. We were in our 30s, so I would say we were long on passion and vision for the project handed us, and a little short on experience in the ways the foundation's program needed to unfold.

Hank and Eileen were a farm team in the truest sense of the word. Together the two would mend fences, build bridges, plow, plant, cultivate, and harvest the crops. It should be noted here that since the farm is representative of a small family farm, the crops serve two purposes. They provide most of the feed eaten by the farm animals and demonstrated how the land produced food.

Hank, as the son of Alice's farm manager Henry Xander Sr., called Hard Bargain home. He was born at Hard Bargain and schooled in agriculture by his father. He was raised among neighbor children and worked for Alice and Henry. Hank Jr. knew everybody in Accokeek. Until his retirement in 2006, he had only spent a few years of his life away from Hard Bargain when he served in the U. S. Navy.

It was a treat to tour the farm with Hank. Wearing his trademark blue jeans and plaid shirt, he had a whole other style of teaching. He would tell tales of growing up at Hard Bargain and the chores that he did alongside his dad. He taught all of us to drive the tractor, was charged with making repairs to buildings and farm equipment that needed attention and informed us when we needed to know about some aspect of the farm.

We all enjoyed his stories of growing up and working for Henry Ferguson in the 1960s -- laying fires in the living room for Saturday visits from neighbors, operating the old farm equipment, and keeping the garden the way Alice had liked it. After his father's death, Hank Jr. and his wife Carol moved into the little farmer's cottage and raised their two sons Andy and Mark there.

Hank loved farming, being his own boss, working outdoors, caring for the animals, and facing the challenges that agriculture presented. The community recognized the knowledge and experience he had gathered, and he was often called upon to lend a helping hand with broken machinery, fallen trees, stuck automobiles, and snowplowing. Those things were a given, but if you asked Hank about his job, he would tell you his favorite part was teaching children.

He loved to share the place with fifth graders on overnight trips. I think he was renewed in his love and concern for Hard Bargain each time he shared it with someone. And touring a farm with this farmer proved to be memorable to many children who often shared their appreciation in thank-you notes. Many a neighbor's teenager, including my sons and those of other staff, were trained by Hank. They were often employed at the farm in the summer to help with seasonal chores of getting in the hay, cleaning the barn, and painting buildings. Hank was grateful for their help during the growing season.

Every year when pastures needed mowing Hank knew how to get the vintage International Harvester tractor running. He knew when there was a leaking roof on one of the farm buildings, and also how to care for the deep well pump. When Hank and I considered repairs and renovations to the farm we would make sure any improvements like a new roof whould outlive us. We joked that his knowledge of the place and its functioning was his job security.

One morning around 11:30 I received a call at the overnight lodge to come up to the top of the hill immediately. There was no reason given, but I suspected something unusual had happened. When I arrived, Hank greeted me and asked if I noticed anything missing. He didn't look very concerned, in fact there was a twinkle in his eye. Maybe catching the boss making a blunder offered just a little bit of satisfaction. It took me awhile to notice that my car was missing from its usual, seemingly flat, parking place just outside the farmhouse. It was a second-hand Peugeot. I think the year was 1985. I have tried to put the details of that car out of my mind.

I stood there puzzled and wondered aloud, "Where did it go?" Then Hank began to explain that he was a few hundred yards away at his home in the farmer's cottage having lunch when he heard a loud crash. He couldn't imagine what had happened – but it didn't take long to notice that my car wasn't there!

It seemed that my little Peugeot decided to go for a spin, or better said, a spin and a tumble. The entrance road to the foundation is about a half mile long and is carved into the side of a steep ravine that drops at least 30 feet to a small stream. There are two hairpin curves and no room for passing others. I had parked only 25 yards from one of the steep embankments.

For some reason the car had begun to roll a full two hours after it was parked. Did one of the cows bump it? Those were the days when the cows roamed the hillsides. Oh, how I wished I had checked the brake and gear setting when I parked it that morning. This was well before the days of the gear we know as park. I imagined that the car must have traveled slowly at first but then picked up speed as it rolled over the lawn from my parking spot and toward a steep hill with about an eight-foot drop. My car must have really picked up speed at this juncture before crossing the gravel road and then crashing into the ravine. I walked over the path that it had traversed and found it resting against a sturdy oak tree halfway down, 10 feet from the stream at the bottom. The parking brake was only partially set and I had not left it in gear. Hank was a veteran of the winding entrance road. His responsibilities included road maintenance as well as rescue efforts when folks got stuck. His warnings to slow down and be watchful for cows and people walking were often unheeded, even by me. I dreaded calling home to tell Tom of this mishap, but I had to own up to my mistake. That afternoon, Tom and Hank teamed up and with the help of a tractor, a wench, ropes and chains, they fetched the car from the ravine. The car was totaled. When it hit the tree, it bent the frame.

Fortunately, Tom and Hank showed me compassion. Humbled by this experience I learned to exercise caution and to further respect Hank's down-home wisdom. He always made me chuckle when I asked him to do something that may not have been on his "to do" list. He would reply, "Yes, Boss" and proceed to do his best. He was such a team player that I thought of Hank more of as a brother than just staff. He moved from Accokeek when he retired. I miss Hank.

Eileen Watts was the most steadfast, patient, and science-minded of our three-member team. In fact, now in her early 80s, Eileen is still working at Hard Bargain as a part-time farmer and educator. Her job became whatever needed doing on the farm or in the lodge; teaching, greeting classes, cleaning, mowing pastures, demonstrating milking, and researching. Eileen began working as a naturalist at the farm in 1973. Her job quickly expanded to the barnyard and beyond. She has been part of the organization for more than 40 years.

If I thought the apocalypse was coming or if I had to trek across country in a wagon train and had to choose one person to help me survive, I would choose Eileen Watts. What a woman! She is knowledgeable in all things basic to life. On the farm, her even-keeled approach to managing a herd of cattle, producing food in a garden or on the hoof, are part of her nature. She's a great cook of basic recipes, soups, bone broth, breads. I still make her "amazing raisin cake" and "cowboy cookies" recipes that she clipped from a farm journal. She keeps a storehouse of goodies that are used, reused and recycled many times over: glass jars, string, cardboard, and farm animal medications. She knows just when to fetch and administer. She has the patience and persistence to tackle farm chores. Problems like the weeds in the field that show up year after year never gain advantage because she is ever on the job. Eileen is always prepared for the onslaught. I remember one year she voluntarily signed up for a course on grass identification with the USDA. I can't think of a more tedious job than to stare at blades of grass and then find them in a field guide. But when discussing the course, she showed her natural curiosity and said, "I just want to know what is growing in our pastures and if it is nutritious enough for our cows."

With Eileen at my side, I have baled hay, plucked chickens, helped with worming the cattle, and watched her teach by example. Eileen has the pioneering spirit that built this country. Our lives now are filled with electronic gadgets like fancy phones, computers, and machines that reproduce video images. I'm sure Eileen uses those things when the need arises but when I'm with her, I appreciate the knowledge she has garnered over the years tending the farm fields, herding animals, gardening and educating hundreds of thousands of children. I want to keep in touch because I appreciate the way she journeys though life.

When I became director, Eileen had been newly installed as the dairy manager or caretaker of our new dairy cow named Favor. She prepared for it rigorously and even though she had very little agricultural background, she sought out experts to inform her on the ins and outs of a dairy operation. Favor, our gentle jersey cow, near the end of her productive life as a milk producer, was a perfect candidate for milking with children. Eileen had to master milking, periodic inoculations, and monitoring the health of all the farm animals.

In keeping with our early agreement to help each other I had learned to milk the cow and found it both pleasant and worrisome. Leaning against the warm hide of our cow Favor, my hands would get tired from the repetitive motion. And then I worried that maybe I hadn't emptied her udder completely, which could result in an infection. At other times I was called upon to bale hay or herd cattle from one pasture to another. These were not everyday chores for me, but a pleasant break from office work. We became a good team and occasionally Hank and Eileen would come to the office at the top of the hill to collate newsletters or light a fire in the living room for visitors. When we established our own newsletter, Eileen wrote wonderful farm updates that educated us all.

When checking in on things in the barnyard, I was a voyeur most of the time. But my curiosity often led me to be present for births, harvesting, and vet visits. Every spring there is the anticipation of the birth of new calves, goats, sheep, and pigs. I remember being summoned to the barnyard for the birth of anywhere from 10 to 12 new piglets. I would watch them emerge magically from their mother, get their sea legs under them and waddle over to find their mother's teats. It's heartwarming to watch these tiny newborns climb over each other until finally they tumble into place. The staff and I would watch quietly through the windows of the pig pen and silently root for each one, especially the runt, to find a spare teat. All the while mamma pig is singing to them a tune composed of rhythmic short deep gentle grunts.

Calving time often was more unpredictable. Usually there would be 10 to 14 cows bred by our bull each year. The cycle was interesting to me. This is a timing problem for most farms, because you don't want a calf born in the middle of January. So, the bull is allowed to be with the herd for several months in the fall when he can impregnate the cows. He is then separated from his harem and put in an especially sturdy pen. If all goes well, after nine months calves emerge. Hopefully that is early spring between the months of March and May.

Eileen was very systematic in her record keeping, helping eliminate catastrophe. Her simple calendar posted on the door to her barnyard office tells a wonderful story. I learned to study Eileen's calendar to see what was on the farm docket. There were notations about when animals had been treated, dates that hay was cut or crops planted, when the bull was secured in his pen, and more. Everyone learned to be observant and to contribute to the journal/diary.

Farms have a rhythm that repeats itself each day like the refrain in a music score, because the animals, crops, and buildings need constant attention. At Hard Bargain Hank and Eileen's day always began in the barnyard with feeding the animals, milking the cow, and gathering eggs from the chickens. It didn't matter whether there were school groups visiting. If there were children present on the farm, they would assist with the early morning chores.

I loved the opportunity to leave my office on the hill and go to Eileen's barnyard office. Eileen was more apt to be the record keeper for our farm team. It gave me the opportunity to catch up on the latest news. Her office was tidy but unconventional as empty pickle jugs lined a shelf on one end of the wall awaiting use as containers for fresh milk. Feed bags, string, scratch pads, and a small space heater were the tools of her trade. There was a small filing cabinet tucked in next to the refrigerator, and a desk there though it seldom was occupied. Eileen, with her science background, kept copious notes on crops planted, animals vaccinated, and names of her consultant vets, soil conservation agents and local farmers with whom we bartered.

Inside Eileen's refrigerator were jugs of milk with dated two-by-two-inch note cards used to record the date that container was filled. Eggs were arranged chronologically. We all knew the system and sometimes a shelf was marked with the words, "Take these first." The freezer held similar notations but they pertained to an animal that had been taken to the local butcher shop and packaged for purchase. I didn't tell my kids that we had once eaten meat from our dairy cow. My daughter refused meat pie when she learned it contained one of our bunnies.

I liked visiting the barnyard office which was occupied every morning from 7:30 to 9:00 and noting the reality of Eileen and Hank's life. I would usually arrive after the heavy-duty chores had been completed. My visits were essential to me because it kept me abreast of the latest project and also reminded me of my duty to preserve the farm and understand all its workings. Eileen kept a coffee pot there and so I frequently enjoyed a meeting over morning coffee flavored with fresh cream from the dairy cow. Topics covered were the health of the individual animals, what piece of equipment needed fixing or replacing and, depending on the season, what crops were at what stage. If it was haying time I was invited back to assist, if the cows needed to be rounded up, then that might be my afternoon project. These requests were not frequent but I loved being part of it all.

As our staff grew the coffee klatch in the barnyard office grew. There was only one chair so everyone stood and talked about the coming day. How many children would be visiting? Which school was here for an overnight? Who was on the schedule? It was a most favored meeting place as opposed to my office which was piled high with papers.

CHAPTER 10

The Community Alice Built

I think one of the most interesting aspects of Alice's 1922 purchase of Hard Bargain was her courage in choosing a country place with so many obstacles like muddy winding roads, well water, dilapidated buildings, and no electricity or telephones. I read recently in Alice's book *Adventures in Southern Maryland* about how she lived in a log cabin on the property the summer the farmhouse was being built. Looking at her picture it's hard to imagine that she lived for days in that rustic space, getting water from a rain barrel and refrigerating eggs and milk in a barrel full of sawdust with a chunk of ice in the middle. Alice's book once again made me admire her pioneering spirit.

Today, visitors to the farm arrive via Indian Head Highway which was finished in 1948 only a few years before Alice's death. In the Ferguson's day they had to bring food for the weekend down from their city house. Today Accokeek has two grocery stores. I spoke with Manning Clagget (the Fergusons' next-door neighbor) a few years ago. Manning was only a toddler when Alice built the farmhouse. At the time he was in his 90s. When we spoke, Manning was still driving a car and operating a small real estate business near the highway where he still worked on a limited basis. I asked Manning if he remembered when electricity had come to Accokeek and he immediately replied, "In 1937 and the first poles put in were at our house and the Ferguson house." I'm struck by how much we still take things like running water and electricity for granted. To think that under what I consider difficult circumstances during the 30s and after the war in the 40s, Alice was developing the farm, building another home down the road called Longview, and commuting on rutted roads to reach Hard Bargain.

Alice and Henry were the early explorers from the city, willing to settle in a less settled place. Those that followed them didn't come in wagon trains but they definitely had the same sense of adventure and ability to weather tough times. The little colony they created has continued to attract folk who want their own place, a homestead near enough to a city, and who would not be subdued by a life of suburban conformity. The list of early residents reveals that most were professionals: teachers, scientists, and engineers. The first settlers, (Straus, Wagner, Kenah, Fairley, North, Thornhill, Harris, Gasparovic, Whyte, Hanson, Newman) came after the war in the mid-40s to cobble together homes built with scarce lumber and even scarcer tradesmen. Much of the building materials used to create the Hard Bargain and the first homes in Accokeek were delivered by boat to Bryan Point, where the fishing pier at the National Colonial Farm is now located.

When Tom and I moved here in 1968, we were fortunate to meet many of the early settlers. They mentored us well. We built a simple, very cabin-like small house, unlike what you would find in the suburbs of Washington. We nestled on our five acre plots and came together as a community at the pool, at the amphitheater, and for events at Hard Bargain.

Two of the first families to settle here were the Wagners and the Kenahs. Both families settled in simple homes across the road from the Hard Bargain's front entrance. Each helped shape the foundation and the Moyaone Reserve. They were part of the "gang" who came on weekends in the 30s for volleyball and to play at the river. After the war Alice bought acreage across the road from the farm, now called Bonds Retreat, and later another property which was named Cactus Hill. And that's when the little colony took form.

From 1954 to 1966 the Alice Ferguson Foundation found its legs and remained a meeting ground for the community. I came to know these early residents as our family settled into the neighborhood. As new residents move here a variety of different homes featuring colonial, cape cod, and more modern designs were built. Using his architectural skills, Charlie Wagner frequently advised newcomers on house building. He helped a whole slew of folks build homes that are considered mid-century modern abodes with characteristics similar to Frank Lloyd Wright architecture. Tom and I asked his help with our design. He suggested we add more windows facing south to capture more light and we followed that advice.

Nancy Wagner, Charlie's wife, was one of three charter members of the Alice Ferguson Foundation. She taught in the nursery school at the cottage that Henry helped set up for neighborhood children, and later kindergarten. I think Nancy is most well known as the founder and editor of Smoke Signals, the community newsletter that keeps us all informed. She also became a champion for a better library in Accokeek. The former public library was one room in the old Accokeek Elementary School. We now have a wonderful new library, to which the Alice Ferguson Foundation contributed $50,000. The library has become a cornerstone of our diverse community.

Dick Kenah was part of the early gang and knew Henry through their geological connections. Dick was the treasurer of the foundation when I became director. He was quite diligent with regard to the Foundation's budget, ensuring we stayed within our means. Additionally, I came to respect his artistic talent which was on display in the furniture he made for his home and his creative use of space in the small dwelling he built himself.

The early resident I came to know the best was Dick's wife, Elizabeth Kenah. E as she was called had been Henry's secretary after Alice's passing. She had written much of his correspondence, served as the second president of the foundation from 1955-56, and had implemented some of the early programs. I found her to be very dedicated to keeping up the high standards set by Alice for Hard Bargain.

I was introduced to E Kenah at a meeting of the garden club in the early 1970s. She was a master gardener and president of the club. The daytime club met at the farmhouse, enjoyed a bag lunch and included members from all of Accokeek. This was before I became a naturalist at Hard Bargain. I had joined because of my love of gardening and at the urging of my friend Beth Nicholson.

One of the projects of the club was to maintain the formal garden that Alice had designed and which overlooks the Potomac. E always made sure the memorial garden, where Alice's and Henry's ashes reside was maintained. In the spring, violas sometimes called johnny-jump-ups, were planted and later some summer annuals. E made regular visits to that space to weed and trim the hedge of baby's breath that surrounded Alice's and Henry's grave markers. Her attention to this burial place was her way of honoring them.

I went to E when I first became director to ask if she would mind being interviewed by a newspaper reporter. The foundation's education program desperately needed some publicity. I arranged for someone from a local newspaper to meet E. I expected an article to be published quickly but, in a few weeks, she called me and said that after meeting the reporter she had decided to write an article herself. To me this was one more indication of the high standards she set for the foundation and its governance. As always E did an excellent job. The article was accepted by Maryland Magazine, a glossy publication put out by the state that highlights interesting programs and places to visit. It was a two-page story entitled "Good Times at Hard Bargain Farm". The article talked about Alice's discovery of the farm and the foundation's program to teach children about the environment. She coined the phrase "Good Times" and I internalized that thought about Hard Bargain to the extent that creating and experiencing "Good Times" became a guiding principle for me. It helped me foster the same playful attitude experienced by visitors in Alice's lifetime as I guided staff and board in all our programs.

Not only was E an expert gardener, great writer, and good neighbor, she also supervised arts and craft days in a little room off the back porch of the farmhouse. It was originally set up for the Fergusons' maid or driver to stay in when they were at Hard Bargain and became known as the craft room. That signage remains today. The garden club sponsored a spring flower sale to help support the foundation's projects, and on the day of the sale the road was marked with large crepe paper flowers made in the craft room. E guided the flower-making and recruited local teens (mostly girls) to come for a few hours on a Saturday to make new flowers and refurbish old ones. In those days, there was no need for publicity because the community was so close that everyone knew to come to the farm on the first Saturday in May to purchase plants at the five-car garage. I was not part of the flower-making but I know that almost every teenage girl that grew up in the Moyaone helped with this project. The flowers were kept in a large cardboard box on a top shelf in the craft room and pulled out every spring to guide visitors.

In 1980 I decided to expand the annual flower sale into an farm festival. People wanted to see the entire farm and experience it the way our visiting students did. Since our visitors were going to the barnyard unaccompanied by staff and exploring the garden, it made sense to use that day to share all the things that make Hard Bargain special, including a food wagon on the hill top, wagon rides, becoming acquainted with the farm animals, and festive music.

I often think of some of the weird things we dreamed up to do at the Spring Farm Festival. One in particular comes to mind and that was cow chip bingo. It is a game where visitors buy chances on a bingo board but the playing board is in the pasture. Eileen marked off a grid with lime in a fenced part of the pasture and made a corresponding chart to show which numbers fell on which squares. Game players were to purchase a square and if the cow dropped a load of manure, otherwise known as a cow pie, in the square then you won a prize. I think we handled it like a 50/50 raffle. We had so much fun designing the game and advertising it as a new feature of the Spring Farm Festival. The actual results were not as much fun as the idea, because our cow was either constipated or hadn't eaten enough to produce a winner until late in the day. I can see now many well-fed cows were needed to make the game interesting but it sure produced lots of giggles.

CHAPTER 11

The Amphitheater

In the early 80s, at a June meeting of the board of directors, I threatened to burn down the amphitheater and to pave Alice's formal garden. Though these two entities embodied Alice's interests and her enthusiasm for making Hard Bargain a gathering place, they also required a lot of attention and ours were not getting any. If they were to survive, I needed the board's help. The amphitheater, which lies dormant all winter was buried in leaves and hosting mice in the nearby outhouses. Alice's perennial garden at the farmhouse was sprouting voluminous weeds making the area unattractive for hosting meetings. I didn't expect to get an okay for my drastic proposal, but I was happy to get the board's attention!

I thought it unusual to have a theater on an operating farm but, like everything built at Hard Bargain, Alice had planned it in detail. In her book she recounts how her neighbors were going through some very tough times.

> *"The winter after the big drought in 1930 and the depression were terrible times in Accokeek. The farmers had no corn to husk, no tobacco to strip, no grain, no potatoes, no apples and many of the animals had been slaughtered. The village had no money and there was nothing to eat and nothing to do. Our farm like all farms is a sponge that can absorb unlimited labor...".*

At that point, Alice decided to employ as many out-of-work men as she could from the village. The next step was to go to the bank and ask for a loan. When the bank asked what Alice wanted it for, she explained that it was to be used to employ an entire village all winter. The bank granted the loan and with all local labor the amphitheater was built. In addition, a winding driveway was carved out of the steep ravine to create the driveway which is still used today.

In Alice's day the amphitheater was used for dances but It also became a meeting place for the neighborhood as there was no community center. A cement floor was poured and storm water drains were installed to control runoff that naturally flowed into the ravine. Chestnut logs were used for seating and later families would bring folding chairs and blankets. As I understand it, there were many amateur productions of Gilbert and Sullivan operettas, which became a favorite of Henry Ferguson who often attended wearing his kilt!

By the 60s a simple wooden stage beneath a towering backdrop of trees became the setting for a greater variety of productions including park ranger talks, puppet shows, square dances and simple plays. My children along with many neighbor children participated in summer workshops. Also, In the 60s and 70s our community included several artists and musicians and the Dildine, Odell, and Lawless families would set up a variety of summer programs. It was wonderful to have experienced theatrical performers in the Moyaone take on this task, but by the time I became executive director, programs were being scheduled less and it became obvious that we needed to find a new crew of volunteers.

In the mid-70s the Moyaone Community was populated by many young families with children. On our road alone there were 28 children. With no summer camps or day care nearby we looked for ways to keep our children productively occupied during the summer. Most families registered their kids for the

Accokeek swim team which met at the pool every morning except Sunday until the end of July. It served children between the ages of six and 18. A problem our working mothers had was knowing what to do with their children in the afternoon and finding someone to run the children's theater workshop had become more difficult. The board helped me to recruit volunteers. The farm staff was tasked with the job of hauling away leaves, unclogging drains, and preparing the outhouses for use. Even with the additional help It took several years to pull the theater program together.

Meanwhile neighbors were clamoring for a children's theater workshop. One of the early theater volunteers, Mike Lipman, friend of board member and later Foundation President Caroline Beane, took on the role of children's theater director/producer. In 1981 he wrote and directed a variety show with music, dance, drama, and comedy. Mike attracted some new talent and the name was changed to Theater in the Woods. In 1984, Peggy DeStefanis and Mickey Oyler created an adult theater group called the Hard Bargain Players. Peggy, chair of the nursing department at the College of Southern Maryland, had two school age children and was a great organizer. Mickey was a music teacher and choir director at the local middle school where she had produced and directed plays for a number of years.

Peggy and Mickey put their heads together, enlisted the aid of interested neighbors and formalized the new group of Hard Bargain Players. This group initially included 3 teachers, a local judge, a lobbyist, artist, a nurse, choir director, two grad students, and various teens and adults who tried out for supporting roles. They produced one act plays, musical reviews, and several original plays from local playwrights. The Players took over the children's theater workshop and recruited guest directors for the summer productions. Their taking over this task was a huge help to me and our community.

The Moyaone community has always attracted artists and environmentalists who quickly supported the theater with patronage and participation. The theater itself was a warm and welcoming hideaway. Although placed near the main entrance to Hard Bargain Farm, it gave the feeling of being ensconced in the deep woods. Weekend evenings in late spring, summer, and early fall often saw neighbors carrying comfortable chairs walking down the winding path to the theater floor where they shared cool drinks and socializing with friends and neighbors as they waited for the show to begin.

Because the community wanted more, Peggy and Mickey enlisted the aid of Moyaone resident Grace Griffith. Grace was a talented and well-known singer and musician in the Washington metropolitan area and she led the season with *Hazelwood*, her own Irish folk group. She invited other musical groups in the area to perform at our theater. This quickly became known as *Concert in the Woods*, where on alternating weeks in the summer, music became a drawing card. Some of the groups who entertained included Kathleen Gotzmer with the *Mill-Run Dulcimer Band*, Lynn Hollyfield and Nina Spruill as *Hollyfield and Spruill*, and Grace Griffith with *Connemara*. Later a local band called *Runty and the Amazons* was formed, with Lynn Hollyfield, Grace Griffith, Nina Spruill, Kevin Kirby, and Jeff Harding. They displayed great rhythm and lots of spunk. Many more musical groups followed and these talented artists have generously provided programs which supported the work of the foundation.

Lynn Hollyfield & Grace Griffith

As time passed the simple wooden stage needed additional development for all the activities, including backdrops for different stage settings, back stage platforms, and storage areas for various artists props. One cool November weekend after a fall production at the theater, the players, their family members, and other volunteers erected a storage shed. The Players brought pots of hot soup and cool drinks and neighbors worked with them for two and a half days from morning to early evening. This was their theater and I know that Alice was somewhere watching her dreams being realized with a new cast of characters.

One neighbor, Jean Thompson (later a board member and president of the foundation), asked for an evening of classical music and financially supported the venture. Other community members offered support as well, some on stage and some back stage, preparing the theater for productions, creating sets, and selling refreshments during productions. Peggy DeStefanis was reminiscing with me recently about her time leading the "Players."

She said, "the truth is that those of us who were the Hard Bargain Players enjoyed it even more than the audience; we enjoyed the time, the friendship, the ambiance and the beer.... I know that still exists today with a little more professionalism from the younger generation who are real theater folk"

Here's a poem by the newsletter editor, Jane Klemer, that captures the atmosphere in our little version of Wolf Trap.

Concert in the Woods II

Crickets and Katydids
Augment the guitars.
A little night music.

Needless to say, I'm ever grateful that board members in that meeting in the early 80s did not agree with my threat to burn the amphitheater and pave Alice's garden!

CHAPTER 12

Oktoberfest

As the new director, I solicited ideas from Moyaone friends and neighbors as to how we could raise money for our environmental education projects. A neighbor, Stafford Allison, suggested an Oktoberfest. Though his profession was as a general contractor, he had been helping cook for a local festival at the German Orphan Home Foundation. His suggestion to bring some of that light-hearted Bavarian music and dance to our neighborhood seemed a perfect fit, so in September 1980 we added an Oktoberfest to the list of special events that opened the farm to the public.

Stafford was very generous with his time as a volunteer in the community and he offered to head up the cooking crew. Now we needed entertainment and I remembered Stafford saying, "We have Germans in the community, why don't you ask them where we can find dancers." I did that and I found that Moyaone neighbors, the Hibbens and Edlers, were active in the "Alt-Washingtonia Schuhplattlers", a group known as the original Bavarian dance group in Washington. Perfect!

At my request Dietlinde Hibben proceeded to contact Nancy and Dave Rosenberg, the organizers of the Schuhplattlers. By the time we decided to host an Oktoberfest it was a bit late in the season. Fitting into the dancers' performance schedule became a challenge. Because Fall is also a very busy time at Hard Bargain with school field trips starting, new staff being trained, and the harvest season underway, we felt fortunate to get the Schuhplattlers and gifted local cooks to offer their talents for our benefit.

Stafford Allison

As we prepared for our first "fest", our staff scrambled to set up a decent dance floor on the deck of the overnight lodge. Nails and rough wooden decking would not be optimum. So, Hank, with help from all, doctored the deck and took down the deck railings to create a stage. Then with volunteer and staff help they moved every picnic table they could find to the surrounding lodge lawn. Ultimately, the overnight lodge set into the hillside with the deck as a stage became a favorite venue of the Schuhplattlers.

In the first few years Stafford offered his hobby kitchen, located in part of his two-car garage, for cooking purposes. The kitchen was furnished with an industrial sized gas stove and large refrigerator. Preparation took nearly a week and I remember that time well. Gathering in his kitchen the night before the festival we cooked up our first German feast and the aroma of onions and sauerkraut mingled with the fall air. There were great vats of German potato salad and sauerkraut being stirred with special wooden paddles that were carved and shaped in Stafford's workshop. It took strong men and a step ladder using these paddles to mix and cook these German favorites.

For many years in the early fall our staff, our board of directors, and other volunteers helped to peel the mountain of onions. Stafford's loyal kitchen crew of Jesse Graybill, John Schlosser, Pete Williams, Herb Savage, Tom Powell and John Hollyfield prepared and served the food. I think we generally used 50 pounds of onions. The Foundation President, Bud Biles, always brought his swim goggles to wear while peeling onions. It was a jolly time and our food samplings were supplemented with special treats of German wursts, blood pudding and stinky cheeses from the famous German sausage maker Egon Bienkert of Baltimore. Bienkert and his family are the sausage makers that provide bratwurst and sauerkraut for Oktoberfests all over the region. Oh, yes, and the German Beer, Spaten on tap, was special ordered by another neighbor, Peter Strauss. To say we had lots of resourceful and talented neighbors lurking in the woods of Accokeek is an understatement.

Our farm staff often joined in the fun with equal gusto. Eileen Watts, with the assistance of school children gathered apples from Hard Bargain's orchard; guests at the event helped press fresh cider from those apples using the foundation's antique press. Hank and some staff gave wagon rides, and many members donated baked goods and crafts that were sold in a little gazebo that had been constructed as a volunteer project by the Crescent Cities Jaycees.

Doris Sharp, another of our talented staff members and native German, taught us how to cook and bake authentic apple strudel. I liked helping with this tasty dessert which required bushels of peeled apples, phyllo dough, sugar, cinnamon, cream, and almonds. We would bake it to perfection in Stafford's kitchen and reheat it the day of the event. Our crew of five or six turned out more than 100 individual strudel servings. The kitchen smelled delicious and as a treat we sampled our work, Yum!

In 2016 the Farm hosted its 36th Annual Oktoberfest with the Schuhplattlers performing. The Oktoberfest became so popular and drew such a crowd that we often had special guests: two Maryland Governors, Schaefer and Glendenning, Congressman Hoyer, State Senator Mike Miller and Delegate Jim Proctor. After managing the event for at least 25 years Stafford Allison was anointed the official 'Oktoberfestmeister.' His loyal crew retired from cooking several years ago. However, the Hard Bargain Oktoberfest still brought together folks from afar, uniting our community and supporting the environmental education program.

Meanwhile, the Hibbens and Edlers, our resident Schuhplattler families enticed the dance group into having their annual Thanksgiving celebration at the overnight lodge. In those days their celebration took place the Saturday after Thanksgiving with many families spending the night and getting a hay ride from Kent Hibben, one of our farm hands and a dancer. Dave Rosenberg, the leader and paternal guardian of the group welcomed Tom and me to those gatherings. There were contests like log sawing and target shooting, and I remember the fun everyone was having as they tested their skills. After a fabulous pot luck dinner we all learned new folk dances from other countries.

Dave Rosenberg

Dave, one of the best huggers I have known, always had a bag of treasures to hand out. He took me aside one Saturday and said, "Kay, you do a great job here and I want to present you with a diamond ring." I thought he said diamond but I knew he was a joker and waited for the punch line. Then he took from his pocket a plain metal ring purchased from a craft store and mounted on top was a dime. It was a dime-on-ring. We laughed together. I gathered several of those rings over the years as did most of his women helpers. He also made macramé key rings but the real gift of Dave was his warm smile and love-filled hugs. Dave passed away in 2005 and every year around Oktoberfest time I think of how he showed us the way to have a rousting good time. The dancers became part of our Hard Bargain Family.

Hard Bargain Staff 1987 – (L to R) Hank Xander, Eileen Watts, Evelyn Biles, Kay Powell, Le Etta Townsend, Cy Adams, Millie Kriemelmeyer, Meryl Lee Hall, Doris Sharp, Barbara Kirkconnell, Arlene Rosenbusch, Erin Watts, Chris Swarth

CHAPTER 13

Gathering Support

Because refurbishing the farm and all the buildings was a top priority, one day in my first year I asked Hank to count buildings on the property. He reported that there were 52 which included small sheds, the amphitheater, animal pens, and even the little building that held the bowling pins and balls for lawn bowling in the years the Fergusons lived there. Though some of those buildings are gone now, money, or I should say lack of it, influenced our choices on which buildings to preserve. Of course, Alice's lovely farmhouse was at the top of the list.

Income from the farm (sale of hay, corn, and calves), fees charged students, member contributions, and endowment income did not begin to cover expenses for maintenancc of the property. Though my predecessor, Bernie, had done a wonderful job in getting an overnight lodge built and establishing a cooperative program with the local school systems of Charles and Prince George's Counties, it was clear that we needed additional funding. The funds to build the overnight lodge had been taken directly from the endowment left by Henry Ferguson. This reduced the income available for maintenance and operation of the education program.

I knew I needed to tackle the job on multiple levels. Before I was hired, I had filled out a grant application for general operating support from the Institute of Museum Services (IMS). It was a generous grant that awarded 10 percent of an organization's operating budget. That meant with the foundation's budget hovering around $100,000, and if the organization qualified, we could get almost $10,000 for running the program which would free up other money for building maintenance.

We had to be declared a museum and it surprised me to discover that zoos and living history farms are considered museums. Not-for-profit institutions that serve the general public by educating in a particular field also met those guidelines. I also learned through my first failed application, that you could get feedback from IMS, and also sample winning applications. Le Etta and I went to work putting a new application together.

Outside funding from other organizations is like a credit rating in the grant world. If you have broad support, then you are presumed to have a cause worth funding. One thing I found lacking in my first application was a failure to show support from other sources. While we worked on numerous grant applications, we needed to gather support from other sources.

At the time, our insurance agent Rob Price was a member of the Crescent Cities Jaycees, an organization of young business men (35 and under) who take on volunteer projects in the community. He suggested I try to get some small farm project approved and if successful they would give up to $1,000, plus labor to help. Our environmental program was well known by the Crescent Cities Jaycees who are headquartered in Charles County. In fact, some members of their families had come to Hard Bargain on school field trips. Our request was approved and we were awarded $1,000 for a maintenance project on the farm. Each year thereafter the Jaycees happily showed up to build, restore, or refurbish something.

An early contribution was a spring-fed watering system. And what is that? The cattle roamed freely all over the farm, even in front of the farmhouse on top of the hill. They drank gallons of water a day and we only had running water at the barn and at the cabin. Hank pointed out there was also evidence of several natural springs running out of the hillside below the cabin where mud puddles accumulated. Once the cows got in the muck the water was no good for drinking. To remedy the problem of providing enough water, an old clawfoot bathtub was placed at the bottom of the hill and was filled by a long string of hoses from the farm's well.

The Soil Conservation Service farm consultants who were great at helping us institute good conservation practices, later offered a solution. They recommended digging trenches and laying perforated pipe to collect the water. The water flowed down out of the hillside and could be collected in a tank. The water flowed constantly so there was no trouble with sediment, mosquitoes, or algae. Excess was channeled into a paved ditch alongside the road and into the swamp. The Jaycees were fascinated by this project and were happy to help engineer and complete more projects.

Every year we proposed a farm improvement that used their talents. They built a gazebo near the lodge, benches for the amphitheater, and a pole building that served as a tractor shed. Because the Jaycees had daytime jobs, most of these tasks were completed over weekends which meant extra work for farm staff. But contributions were so valuable that it was worth every minute. We grew to love the Jaycees, and many of the same people would show up time after time. They were talented men who gave freely.

After several years of help from Jaycees, figuring out ways to document the support we received from the National Park Service, and also advice from Scott Odell, a member who was familiar with IMS, we finally won a grant. The day the letter arrived announcing our success was one of the brightest highlights I experienced in my career. Our $90,000-plus budget would be increased by $9,900. We had cracked at least one code to improving our program and securing the future of the foundation. That first grant was followed with general support grants. for two more years

To me the farmhouse felt more like a residence than a foundation headquarters and I liked it that way. It reminded me that Hard Bargain was special and had to be protected. Occasionally I would wander through the house inspecting the pantry full of precious dishes, and paging though books in the living room. The volleyball net and volleyball were still in the cabinet by the front door - the ball deflated and the net dry-rotted - still in place ten or more years after Henry's passing.

The Institute of Museum Services also solicited grant applications for special preservation projects and I thought we could secure one for the Ferguson memorabilia. We applied and happily were approved for special project support enabling us to preserve and archive all the photos, papers, and documents associated with Alice's and Henry's life at Hard Bargain. That grant was received in 1986. Its purpose was to catalogue and preserve an immense collection of books, photos, letters, and documents that we named the Ferguson Collection. Many of these items had been stored in the attic in cardboard boxes and exposed to heat and cold as the seasons changed.

Mrs. Xander had retired by this time and there was no one living in the house. Taking care of household duties and preparing for meetings was left to Le Etta and me. Managing the house became a burden. I hoped to find someone with the skills to preserve the collection and perhaps live upstairs in the house, so I turned to our community. Dietlinde Hibben (you met her earlier as a dancer) responded to my inquiry. I offered her the position if she would be willing to live in the house while she worked on the project and take that as part of her salary. She was delighted. Dietlinde was artistic, very organized, and with a little training became the perfect person to work on preserving the material. She created special acid proof folders for documents and photos, being sure to wear her white gloves when handling all of it.

We had already hired Doris Sharp to work part time on the project. I met Doris when we co-chaired a July 4 pool party. Doris lived nearby and her sons were on the swim team. She told me that she was looking for part-time work so I invited her to apply to work with Dietlinde on the conservation of the

Ferguson papers. Doris was also a German native so she and Dietlinde seemed the perfect team to accomplish this task. You could often hear them conversing in their native German, then silence. Sometimes laughter poured out of the newly created library. They were a good team. The job was done superbly, and a lasting friendship created between the two families. Dietlinde's children were grateful to have Mom nearby and their oldest son Kent worked on the farm in summers and eventually served on the board of directors.

Dietlinde, Doris & Le Etta

Working with Doris, I discovered a delightful person with a great sense of humor. When Doris joined the staff, she didn't have any formal training in environment science, agriculture, computers, or cooking. But she adapted to our small staff and became one of our most versatile employees. Doris happened to join the staff the same year we purchased our first computer. Up until that time we were using typewriters, carbon paper copies, and a mimeograph machine. Large copying projects were taken to the community college or a local printer's office. That year Doris helped in the educational program and also, with Le Etta's help, used the new computer to record information concerning the Ferguson Collection.

Doris proved to be an eager learner who honored the Hard Bargain's past and tackled anything put on her plate. This made for an interesting position description. She was our chief gardener, office assistant, and cataloguer of Ferguson memorabilia, newsletter compiler, special activities coordinator, caterer at meetings, and birthday cake maker. In the late 80s our staff was so small that each of us would get a specially baked birthday cake at lunch. Doris used her creativity and whatever she had on hand to create the cakes. They also came with funny names. My favorite was "humble crumble". Doris was a key member of the staff until she retired to North Carolina in 2016. Over her 30 years of service to the foundation, she became the resident historian and developed deep connections in the community.

CHAPTER 14

Building a Foundation to Educate Youth

In 1969, the foundation initiated a cooperative educational program. The National Park Service funded park rangers to teach, the school systems helped develop curriculum and brought students, and the foundation coordinated the field trips and hosted them at Hard Bargain. Ten years later when I became director, it was serving thousands of Maryland students each year with a very modest budget. A priority was to get the word out that the education program was alive and well. Here is a little history of how the program evolved.

It actually begins with Alice and Henry and the friends they attracted after World War II. These early residents were eager to protect the acres of woods, fields, and streams in the area. That ideal was imbedded in the way they lived. As Pat Vanderslice wrote in her 1989 history on the occasion of the twentieth anniversary of the education program, "It seems that environmentalists were incubating in Accokeek even before Rachel Carson's Silent Spring was published in 1962." A natural outcome to the creation of the foundation was a focus on the environment. The Moyaone community embraced the concept of a nature education program. Many didn't know what had been developed.

Those early residents were still imagining Hard Bargain the way they had experienced it when Henry and Alice were living there.

An identity crisis existed because the education program was hidden from the public at large. When I spoke with residents, I discovered that the connection a person had with the Alice Ferguson Foundation determined their idea of its purpose. I wanted everyone to focus on the good work we were doing using the farm and surrounding environment as teaching tools.

The outdated view that Hard Bargain was just a playground for viewing fireworks on July 4, sledding in the winter, being entertained in the amphitheater, and the flower sale was not serving the needs of the organization. It wasn't unusual for neighbors to come to the farmhouse unannounced with visitors, walk into the living room and show them the view of Mount Vernon and the wonderful furnishings. Maybe they had attended parties hosted by Alice and Henry. And for these folks Hard Bargain still felt like a "good times" place. I handled this very gently because we needed all the community support we could muster. Also, I didn't want to disturb the kind of reverence they had for Hard Bargain. I considered it an asset. Expanding that viewpoint took time.

One outrageous example of this casual attitude occurred early in my tenure and involved a politician. It turned into a nightmare for me, at least for one day. In the early 80s we had a Republican County Executive named Larry Hogan, father of the current the governor of Maryland. Mr. Hogan had been newly elected in the majority Democratic Prince George's County. Soon after his election we got a call from Mr. Hogan's office. The foundation was listed as a retreat center. Mr. Hogan wanted to hold a secret retreat somewhere in the county with his newly-elected and appointed council.

I was surprised and thrilled. However, we only offered our overnight lodge. It was equipped with metal bunk beds from surplus property and the foundation usually hosted scout groups on the weekends. It wasn't comfortable for adults. We made this clear, the retreat was scheduled and we were instructed to keep it mum. So, we did and prepared as best we could. It was October and there was lots of buzz in the press about Mr. Hogan's upset of the Democratic candidate. I had some fantasy that he would love Hard Bargain, help promote us and maybe even put us in the county budget. The weekend came and there were two big pieces of local news. The first was a predicted northeaster that might hit our area and the other was the mysterious location of the new county executive's retreat. I thought we could carry this off, but I was nervous.

They arrived on a Friday afternoon prepared to stay two nights. The storm hit in the mid-afternoon just when Mr. Hogan's advisors were getting settled. There were lots of trees down all over Accokeek which resulted in a big power outage. We not only had no electricity but also no water because our deep well has an electric pump. I called Al Korzan, my closest contact in the National Park Service at Fort Washington and asked if they could furnish a generator. Sure, enough this retreat had gotten so much press that the park service immediately delivered a very large generator. It was a big noisy thing, but I was relieved that the show would go on. The next morning Mr. Hogan and his associates took us up on our offer of a short tour of the farm. I took them to the barnyard where Eileen Watts instructed them in cow milking. Afterward they headed for more comfortable surroundings in the farmhouse.

Things were going well considering the weather and continuing power outage. The longer they were on the premises the more I fantasized that we would be given a place in the budget. Then we had a surprise visitor. One of our more volatile neighbors, Ken Otis, showed up at the front door looking for Hank to help him clear a large tree off Bonds Retreat Road. It completely blocked the road and our neighbors were trapped. I asked Ken, who could be loud, to please quiet down because Mr. Hogan was holding a meeting in the living room. Ken didn't even pause. To my horror he pulled aside the curtains in the doorway, interrupted the meeting by demanding the county executive needed to put aside all their business and get our roads cleared. He declared that only the county could handle this job. I could have cried. Here we were trying to shelter our county's new politicians, introduce them to Hard Bargain and gain footing. I never forgave Ken for the intrusion and at any rate it wouldn't have done any good to try to get him to understand my outrage. The tree was removed and that was what was important to him.

We did get one small donation from Mr. Hogan. It seems that his family liked to ride horses and he wanted to donate one to the farm. Hank, Eileen, and I drove to his home on Central Avenue and loaded the horse into our trailer and brought him back to the farm. Then I thought, "Oh good, we can care for his horse, the kids visiting will enjoy it, and the farm will have a connection." We never heard from Mr. Hogan and furthermore we had the expense of an old horse to show for our efforts. I learned that we needed to find better ways to court our politicians and to feather our nest!

Another problem was that there are two operating farms, managed by two foundations on Bryan Point Road in Accokeek, and each is managed by a private foundation for educational purposes. So, if you said, "I'm going to the farm" it could mean one of two places. In the early 70s each farm was managed informally, hence no locked gates or security checks. One evening Tom and I were having dinner with neighbors, Bill and Clara Moran. Bill Moran served on the board of the Accokeek Foundation and was public affairs chairman of the Moyaone association. His wife Clara worked at the Colonial Farm. They kept mentioning "the farm" and I knew instantly that their reference to farm meant different things to each of us.

Those who knew the Fergusons or had worked or played there would be referring to "the farm" as Hard Bargain which was operated by the Alice Ferguson Foundation. Those locals, who had helped establish Piscataway Park, were more closely aligned with the National Colonial Farm. So, in that case "the farm" meant the Colonial Farm located less than a mile from Hard Bargain at the end of Bryan Point Road and operated by the Accokeek Foundation. The Accokeek Foundation was formed to help create the park. The establishment of the Piscataway Park had divided the community because many didn't want federal government interference in their neighborhood. Hence, whatever farm you were associated with could infer a political point of view, for or against the establishment of Piscataway Park. Fortunately, that is history now. Another distinction had to be made and that was with the schools we hosted. Hard Bargain was more than a farm to the students who visited for overnight field trips. Our foundation had a co-operative educational program with Charles and Prince George's Counties. By the time I arrived these programs were entrenched to such an extent that the school systems had made the field trips part of their science curriculum, teaching about the food web, decomposition, and farm life. A staff person from each school system was present for all the fifth-grade overnight field trips.

John Neville, supervisor of environmental education for Prince George's County, arranged for a member of his staff to be present to assist the teacher and chaperones. In Charles County, Will Harr, science supervisor, would coordinate field trips and Bob Morrow, a physical education teacher accompanied each class to help with campfires and be a chaperone overnight. Charles County was small enough so that Hard Bargain could host every fifth-grade class. It was a high point for those students and they looked forward to it.

These programs were very effective because staff from each county worked closely with us and often the teacher/student ratio was one to six. It was truly a hands-on experience. In Prince George's County we were known as the Ferguson Farm. The Charles County students called us Hard Bargain Farm.

The challenge was to decide how to have one identity and claim it in such a way that we could get more support from our membership, recognition for our educational program, and funding from other sources. As much as we respected and appreciated the significant help we received from each county, it didn't provide enough support to keep the farm going. The foundation had a small brochure but it was not widely distributed and the farm had no logo. The original brochure had a picture of cows on the front and spoke of the farm and a few nature trails.

There was also the Max North Nature Trail brochure. But neither publication expressed what our organization was actually teaching. Eventually our small part-time staff collaborated on ideas for a name and we also spent time looking at other organizations. We decided to abandon the reference to Ferguson

Doris, Eileen & friends

Farm although there are still those that think of us that way. We settled on Hard Bargain Farm Environmental Center, owned and operated by the Alice Ferguson Foundation. That enlarged our image and separated us from the National Colonial Farm.

This also later positioned us for establishment of the Potomac River Program. It may seem that this was always our image, but education about the environment was not as large a focus in those days, so to graduate from farm and nature trail to environmental center was a leap.

In this instance we were helped by our local politicians. Delegate Jim Proctor had worked in the school system, and as a principal of Kettering Elementary he had come with classes to Hard Bargain and even spent the night in the lodge. Senator Mike Miller also advocated for our program. Mike had ancestral connections to Accokeek and Bryan Point. Evidently some of his relatives had lived there and he is a student of that history. Later, Mac Middleton, chair of the Charles County Commissioners, joined this team of elected officials to help us get support.

To give you a feel for those days I'm sharing a poem written by one of the Charles County fifth grade classes in 1981.

Oh, Mrs. Ferguson Had A Farm

Oh, Mrs. Ferguson had a farm,
And she made it nice,
She loaded it with animals,
Goats, horses, cows and mice.

And on that farm, we milked a cow,
We even snatched some eggs,
We fed the hungry pigs some slop,
And scratched the big fat sow.

And on that farm, we took a trail,
We saw a water snake,
We slipped and landed in the marsh,
Where we all did flail.

And on that farm, we flopped in hay,
Itching every which a-way,
And the wagon we did ride,
We had a perfect day.

And at night the fire did crack,
We roasted marshmallows,
We told some stories one by one,
So scary walking back.

So thank you Mrs. Ferguson,
For a lot of fun,
We really do appreciate,
Everything kind you've done.

From J.C. Parks Elementary School Fifth grade class

In 1982, three years into my job as executive director, we held an environmental education conference at Hard Bargain. Our Foundation President, Elmer Biles, pushed for a conference and frankly, I was overwhelmed by the thought of having a team of environmentalists come there to evaluate our program. The trails were subpar; our building maintenance was lacking, and most of all I was afraid that it would be revealed that I, Kay Powell, sociology major, was running an environmental program. There was so much to do and I felt like I was being forced to entertain unexpected house guests. I needed to have everything in order, which seemed impossible.

In spite of my fears, I trusted our foundation president's wisdom and experience. The conference was held in October and was chaired by Belva Jensen, professor emeritus of Charles County Community College and a very active resident of the Moyaone community. Among the organizations sending participants were the National Parks and Conservation Association, the National Park Service, Patuxent River Park, Maryland National Capital Parks, the Chesapeake Bay Foundation, and Maryland Department of Education. It was very empowering to be in the presence of these folks who later became allies of the foundation.

Near the end of our conference we had a different kind of uninvited guest. A bat flew down out of the farmhouse chimney and rested on the mantle of the fireplace. These avid naturalists were not in the least bit frightened. They were more intrigued with its identification and removing it safely. Someone fetched a dip net, captured and released it. That brought an end to the meeting so we moved on to conversation and refreshments.

In all my worry about having things just right, I neglected to take into account the effect that Hard Bargain would have on them. Driving up to the top of the hill and seeing the view of the Potomac and then experiencing the charm of the farmhouse totally enchanted them.

Our work was beginning to pay off. The next year, Hard Bargain Farm was selected to represent the State of Maryland in the National Search for Excellence in Science Education. We won first place, chosen by the Maryland Association of Science Teachers and the Maryland State Department of Education. Our program was recognized throughout Maryland as having an exemplary science program in a non-school setting. Our staff and board were so proud and this recognition proved to be something to build on.

CHAPTER 15

Potomac River Program

By the mid-80s, my staff and I came to realize that our location right on the Potomac River was a big plus and we weren't taking advantage of it. We were studying the Potomac in small ways like showing students the aquatic life in Accokeek Creek and the swamps and marshes near the river, but our education program featured the farm more than the river.

The Chesapeake Bay Foundation was getting a lot of accolades for its work cleaning up and protecting the Chesapeake and its estuaries. I studied their brochures and annual reports to figure out how they supported their program and found that they were getting broad-based support and a grant from the state. I went to Annapolis to look at the state budget and sure enough there was a line item for the Chesapeake Bay Foundation. I discovered that the State of Maryland supports outreach programs that teach the school curriculum.

I made an appointment to meet with Don Baugh, the education coordinator for the Bay Foundation. Don was warm and engaging and I was impressed with his generosity about the details of their program and how they received state support. I can't rave enough about these organizations and their educators. Meeting with them and sharing information taught me that there can never be too many organizations or individuals teaching about ecology and caring for our planet.

Before I met Don, I worried that I would be viewed as competition for a limited pot of money. That was far from the truth and ultimately their model encouraged me to be more generous with others trying to make their mark in this area of environmental education. Don and I, as well as representatives of the National Aquarium, became friends and checked in on each other as we navigated the funding cycles and the state standards set for us.

In 1986, our State Senator Mike Miller and our local delegates Gary Alexander, Joe Vallario and Bill McCaffery were successful in getting state support for the foundation. This funding established our Potomac River Program and allowed us to have a full-time biologist/educator to develop a curriculum that meshed with the state curriculum standards. It was the step forward we needed to sustain the environmental educational program for years to come. The establishment of the Potomac River Program with funding from the state presented us with new opportunities.

Steny Hoyer, Nancy Wagner & Mike Miller

Every single school day at the farm was filled to capacity with field trips and there was a waiting list. Hosting so many visitors was hard on the farm's aging buildings, the barnyard animals, and nature trails. It was also a challenge to schedule our part-time staff. In the spring and fall when we were the busiest, I would lose office staff to the program. Everyone was teaching. We loved our program and we wanted to share it without depleting what we had built. It seemed reasonable to expand our program with the National Park Service and the Maryland education community.

The foundation shifted its primary focus from the farm to the Potomac River and developed educational activities that helped protect it. Christopher Swarth the new director of that program came to me one day and suggested we partner with other groups to clean up the shoreline. By the late 80s, litter had ruined the pristine sandy shoreline. Garbage from the city like plastic cups, glass bottles, old clothing, and even tires accumulated on the beach as it traveled downstream.

I remember being hesitant to start this project because our staff was already working many weekends. It meant giving up another Saturday and committing to one more annual event. All our staff had young families and we tried to save the weekends to be with them. However, I agreed with Chris that it didn't seem right that we would be teaching environmental conservation and not have a plan in place to take care of our own backyard.

Then one Saturday permanently changed the way I tunderstood the Foundation's Environmental Program. It was the Third Annual Potomac River Cleanup. My job at special events like this was to get media attention and host local dignitaries to help raise awareness of the river's problems. On this day I was waiting for the Prince George's County Executive Parris Glendenning.

Mr. Glendenning was a very environmentally conscious leader who recognized that a clean Potomac could enhance the life of our county's citizens. He asked if he could bring Raymond, his 10-year-old son, to help with the cleanup. It was and still is a perfect family project and there were many scouts, families, and friends helping out. I imagine it was like those days when Alice lined up farm and garden chores for her city visitors.

I was anticipating some good news coverage and an opportunity to get to know the county executive better. The wait was longer than expected so I decided to use the time by cleaning one small part of shoreline near our meeting place. The spot I chose was only about two square feet and my challenge was to see if I could completely clean it of all litter. The predominant item was small pieces of Styrofoam, the plastic used in packing and for disposable cups. This is one of the worst kinds of trash because it never goes away and in this particular spot each piece was about the size of a pea. When dropped outdoors after use, Styrofoam crumbles but never decays. Unfortunately, fish and birds mistake it for food so it is also a hazard to the wildlife.

As I began to pick up these tiny pieces, I could see it would be a tedious job. Some pieces were really dirty but I wore gloves. As I worked, the shape and feel of this spongy plastic intermingled with sand and seaweed and the volume of this litter became more disturbing. It was probably as bad as removing a needle in a haystack because I could see the plastics but it was hard to pick up the grimy little pieces. After about twenty minutes I realized it would take more time and effort. I was nowhere near purging my chosen spot.

I halted my effort when Mr. Glendenning and his son arrived. He and Raymond had a great time pulling out old tires, another ghastly way the river is used as a dumping ground. We got some wonderful pictures of Raymond rolling a large dirty old tire out of the water up onto dry land. Parris later asked for a copy of the picture and I understand that he kept it on his desk for a long time. Parris later became governor of Maryland and never forgot his visit to Hard Bargain.

Not long after the cleanup, I was attending another event where they were serving juice and coffee in Styrofoam cups. As soon as I took hold of that cup, I knew I could never drink from a Styrofoam cup again. I was reliving that day on the spoiled beach. More than 20 years later, I still cringe when for some reason I have to touch and or use the stuff, especially when it is used as packing material. I wish they would ban it.

Director of Environmental Studies Sil Pembleton & pupil

Also, at the cleanup that day I realized the importance of getting our communities involved in these events and I understood that more is happening than cleaning a beach. Of course, the reduction of litter is important, but those kinds of actions bring about an inner awareness that can radically change behavior, just like my experience with Styrofoam.

In 1989, Chris Swarth left the foundation to become the Director of Patuxent River Park. The vacancy created when Chris left gave me the opportunity to hire Seliesa Pembleton, a talented naturalist and educator. Seliesa (Sil's) first affiliation with the foundation occurred in the Spring of 1988 when I hired her on a temporary basis to assist us with curriculum development. In February 1990, she became the first Director of Environmental Studies which encompassed a wide range of responsibilities including creating a variety of new classes for students, training teachers and staff, representing the foundation at environmental conferences and filling in as executive director when I was out of the office. The job was a perfect fit because she had a lot of past experience developing curriculum with school children and working with volunteers.

She expanded the Potomac River cleanup by offering training for the site facilitators and also recruiting more people to take on a larger portion of the watershed. The Potomac Watershed Cleanup became a network of partners from the headwaters to the Chesapeake who felt like friends united in a common goal. We were members of conservation organizations, local, state and federal agencies, and private citizens who cared about the environment and the river. Once the first few years of press got out, people called volunteering to start new sites or to find out where to go to pick up trash. All the national parks on the river joined in.

Within 10 years there were more than 100 sites, all organized by Hard Bargain staff who already had a full- time job. At the end of a cleanup day, wet muddy people would often come by to say "Thanks for having this cleanup. It makes me feel good!" One of the most popular activities she and our staff developed was an one called, "Who Polluted the Potomac?" The activity answered a question we often got from children. It was a reinvention of an activity called "Who dirtied the water?" The materials used are a gallon jug filled with water, and film canisters containing mock pollutants which demonstrate how each person plays a part in pollution. We found funding to reproduce and teach this activity at a Maryland Association of Environmental and Outdoor Education Conference. The activity spread rapidly and one day I received a letter from someone in New Zealand thanking us for sharing the activity, and expressing appreciation of how it helped others understand the complexity of a pollution problem in his country.

In the Fall of 1994, a delegation from Japan visited as part of the Environmental Education and Training Group. Our environmental program had gotten notice and several times a year our facility became a stop-off place for environmental groups visiting from foreign countries. Sil, as the Maryland Coordinator for Project Wild, hosted the group and also introduced them to our "Who Polluted the Potomac." That experience led to an invitation for her to teach hands-on environmental workshops in Japan – all expenses paid. She visited Japan in the Spring of 1994, traveling throughout the country and giving 15 workshops. She again visited in 1997. These exchanges stressed the idea that although an ocean separates us, we all share the waters of the earth and must work together to protect them. In 1999, our environmental expertise was requested once again. Because Sil had other obligations I was honored to be able to accompany Pat McGlashan, another gifted curriculum specialist, to meet staff and park officials at both parks and schools.

I also spoke to 250 park employees at the Olympic Center in Tokyo about our non-profit foundation and how we used volunteers. There were many questions concerning the use of volunteers in organizations like ours. At that point in time the foundation staff continued being stretched to its limit and I wasn't sure what it could sustain in terms of the addition of more programs. A year earlier I had announced my decision to retire in July and this trip opened my eyes to the never-ending need for environmental education worldwide. I didn't answer the call to expand our role and to do more overseas education, a decision I have revisited many times as I watch pollution of our oceans grow.

CHAPTER 16

Environmental Program Gains National Attention

In 1996, we were partnering for the river cleanup with national parks and schools offsite, offering workshops to park rangers and educators and getting grants for those programs. When I think back to how the foundation began and how modest our goals were in the beginning, I never imagined such an outcome. It was wonderful but at the same time our staff had not grown significantly and salaries were subpar. I was both excited and overwhelmed by our success and once again I needed help. We were still a small staff and I had remained responsible for all the fundraising.

One of our volunteers, Tracy Bowen, who lived in the foundation's cottage offered her help. She was knowledgeable of fundraising through connections with political campaigns and seemed eager to work on fundraising and grant applications. Again, to receive grants an organization needs something akin to a credit rating. Those qualities are demonstrated through a diverse support base, a successful education program, and publicity. Tracy learned about a National Sustainability Award being given by Renew America. I recognized the value of that award because early in my tenure, the foundation had been recognized with an award given by the National Science Teachers Association. That recognition had been the stepping stone to the establishment of the Potomac River Program.

Representative Steny Hoyer & the author

There were not many of those recognitions for institutions such as ours. The application process was quite tedious and required extensive documentation, with submission of number of people served, publicity, and curriculum samples. Tracy did a spectacular job submitting information for the award and our foundation won. "Renew America's Award for Environmental Sustainability" was a national recognition and then we served as a model organization.

To show how important the recognition was, I quote our Representative Steny Hoyer's entry into *The Congressional Record* on February 28, 1996.

> *"Mr. Speaker, it is with great pleasure that I rise today to recognize the Alice Ferguson Foundation and the Hard Bargain Farm Environmental Center located in Accokeek, Maryland. On January 23, Hard Bargain Farm was named the winner of Renew America's National Environment Award. This award is part of the 6th annual renew America National Awards for Environmental Sustainability. The awards are given each year to programs throughout the nation that demonstrate leadership and excellence in environmental sustainability."*

> *"I have long been a supporter of the educational programs offered by Hard Bargain Farm and commend them on this selection from a pool of over 1600 applicants in 24 categories. I have been honored to work hand in hand with them throughout the Fifth Congressional District to protect the Potomac River through education efforts, environmental stewardship and conservation action projects.*
>
> *"Mr. Speaker this recognition of Hard Bargain's achievement and dedication to the environment marks two important firsts. Not only is this the first time Renew America has honored a Maryland organization in the institutional education category, but it is also the first time that a National Park Program has received such recognition.*
>
> *"For the past 25 years, Mr. Speaker, Hard Bargain Farm has worked in a unique and highly effective partnership with the National Park Service to develop quality environmental education programs. I commend the leadership and experience of the Alice Ferguson foundation and am very proud to rise today with my colleagues in recognition of this very special award."*

Getting that award felt like receiving an Oscar. We were invited to the White House (actually the ceremony was in the old executive office building next door) but the presentation was made by Hillary Clinton. I thought we had reached the top of the mountain.

Most of the credit has to go to Sil our director of environmental education and her leadership of our highly motivated and capable staff. Here's why. Sil got involved with the Maryland Association of Environmental and Outdoor Education (MAEOE), the Maryland organization that fostered collaboration of all outdoor and environmental educators. She also connected with Gary Heath, Maryland Supervisor of Environmental Education, to learn about the state's environmental education priorities.

Conferences were held annually in the fall at different outdoor centers where staff could sleep overnight and trade program ideas. The group is so large now that meetings are generally held in hotels. In a few years Sil was on the board of directors. Our staff often presented workshops for MAEOE members as they learned to implement curriculum-based education. That sounds like a lot of jargon but what it meant for the farm was that we were able to align the course content in our classes with the curriculum taught at various grade levels.

At the farm it is considered a school day when subject matter in the curriculum is covered and would not be repeated in the classroom. This was revolutionary in the 80s and 90s. Our teaching methods used the scientific method and advanced data collection techniques. This was a time when Maryland was shifting to problem-solving type learning where teams of students would work to find solutions. All these changes in curriculum demonstrated to school officials, teachers, and parents that field trips were both fun excursions, enrichment opportunities, and science lessons.

As an advocate for protecting wildlife and conserving our river, what the foundation was doing in our small programs could transform the way children were taught science and how partnerships could expand learning. The Potomac River Cleanup is a great example of that phenomenon; the cleanup is now 30 years old. It started with two sites and now is held at hundreds of sites from the headwaters in West Virginia to the Chesapeake Bay. It is broadly funded. Foundation staff handled the whole cleanup and were making amazing contacts and associations with people who believed in our educational outreach. We developed close ties with these cooperating organizations and they wanted to create partnerships.

The 1996 Potomac River cleanup was a record breaker when 1,894 volunteers hauled over 137.5 tons of trash from the Potomac and its tributaries in Maryland, Virginia, Washington, D.C., and West Virginia. As we discussed the cleanup, we shared the thought that if all these parks could clean the river together, it was possible that we could educate together. After all, it was the same watershed with the same biology and history. One curriculum could serve us all. By that time, we had met and worked with Julia Washburn a very influential and farsighted National Park Service employee.

Sil and Julia worked extensively together as many of the cleanup sites were in national parks. Sometime in 1997, Sil's and my idea was shared with Julia, the Rock Creek Park chief ranger, and Maggie Zadorozny, a park education specialist. Julia and Maggie had been thinking the same way and decided to pursue funding.

Then one day Sil told me of a phone call she had just received from Julia. The National Parks and Conservation Association had grant funding from the Toyota Corporation to teach science to high school students in the national parks and they were seeking grant proposals. It was a perfect fit. Julia, Maggie, Sil, and I worked one weekend at Rock Creek to write the grant for the current version of Bridging the Watershed Program that serves parks in the region. I knew that if the program was a success our organization with me as executive director, would really be taxed to its limits. Our proposal was to design a science curriculum for high school students using the Potomac River as the focus and to teach things like testing water samples, invasive plant identification and eradication, and trash analysis.

The most exciting element was to train national park rangers and teachers together in workshops each summer so that they could bring their classes to the parks for science study. The whole concept was a partnership between science teachers, park rangers and foundation staff. The workshops were to be held at Hard Bargain for two weeks with some field trips to national parks as part of the training. This was different from our other educational offerings in that Hard Bargain staff was now being funded to teach high school science in the national parks. I remember the last few days before the grant was due. We met at Rock Creek Park in Julia's office and hammered out the details. I worked on the budget and held my breath when I signed the proposal. A new era might be unfolding for the foundation.

A few months later we learned that our new program would be funded and was one of only five in the entire United States. More breath holding from me as we planned a trip to Lowell National Historic Site in Massachusetts. It was a big weekend and we were meeting with really farsighted educators. The project required a fair amount of recordkeeping, hiring a curriculum writer and keeping to our proposed timeline. I had again been assigned the budget oversight and at that time the foundation didn't have outside accounting support. I took on the project but, needless to say, it wasn't long before we hired someone to take on this task.

I was in my 18th year as executive director of the foundation and my management skills were really being tested. I was a good leader for a small staff and could foster creativity but the day-to-day correspondence and project oversight were taxing me to my limits. My one claim to fame in the whole project was that I came up with the name. The parks we worked with were on both sides of the Potomac and had varying natural resources that could be shared among us. Since we were crisscrossing the Potomac I thought about bridges of all kinds and the idea of connecting our resources and bridging the Potomac seemed good. I suggested "Bridging the Watershed" now almost exclusively referred to as "Bridging." In April 2018, Julia, Maggie and I were recognized for "our tireless efforts in promoting hands-on science, collaboration, and student engagement on the occasion of the 20th Anniversary of Bridging the Watershed." Sil, our original team member was living out of state, but we thought of her that day and wished she could be there with us. Ours is a national model for partnerships with the National Park Service and I'm really proud of the part Hard Bargain staff played in its creation.

CHAPTER 17

Keeping the Foundation a "Good Times" Place

When Alice passed away, Henry set up the foundation so that he and others could still have "Good Times" there, more specifically weekend cocktail parties. In those early days, which was the mid-50s, he wrote a one-page essay to those studying possible uses for Hard Bargain titled "Soft Thoughts on Hard Bargain".

Henry begins the piece by writing,

> *"Hard Bargain was built for good times, both for Alice and me and our friends. On occasion I have thought it more for our friends than ourselves."*
>
> *"Without my knowledge but entirely within its rights, the Foundation has assured the long faced gentlemen of the Internal Revenue, whom the slightest suspicion of a good time is an anathema that it shall be turned into an eleemosynary (*charitable or gratuitous) institution of some kind. I don't remember what the statement said, but a junior college, cultural center (presumably dry) and a residence for a stuffy guidance counselor have been suggested. The thought turns my stomach."*

Henry goes on to suggest themes, but they all focus on a meeting place for continued "Good Times." Good times did happen while I was there. For example, Hard Bargain's educational program was designed so that learning didn't preclude having fun. Our staff worked to involve students in lots of hands-on activities. It increased their interest and understanding of the farm and surrounding environment.

In a small publication celebrating the 20th anniversary of the Educational Program, author Pat Vanderslice, my neighbor and fellow staff member, asked "What were the most satisfying aspects of working at Hard Bargain?"

The staff responses to the foundation's environmental program I think are telling. These were their comments:

- Enjoying the natural world with children as a shared experience
- Children's eager response/excitement /discovery
- Being outdoors close to nature/watching seasons change
- Closeness of staff
- Watching students overcome fear of unknown (snakes, insects, large animals and the woods)
- Hay rides
- Introducing children to the joy of living and working on a farm.

Many teachers have made the field trip to Hard Bargain the top event of the school year. One such teacher is Jill Jowdy Morrow, a vivacious woman who has so much enthusiasm that it's contagious to all who work with her. For about 35 years Jill has taught physical education at Glasva Wayside Elementary School in Charles County.

In the early 80s a top priority was to repair and restore the farm's buildings. Jill always wanted to set records and have her students be the best. Here's how she made one fifth grade class trip to Hard Bargain memorable. The log cabin, used for evening campfires by students, was at the top of the list because the logs had deteriorated, and a substantial number needed to be replaced. Mrs. Xander, who had a large stand of pine trees on property she owned, was willing to donate them for this project. Dick Williams, our part-time handyman, and Hank Xander cut the logs and brought them up to the cabin for debarking. We knew this would take a lot of time so we purchased a tool called a draw knife and had classes of children at the cabin work on debarking.

Usually a class would only be able to take the bark off one log. Jill set a goal of having her class debark the most logs. We had only one draw knife with a pine log setup on saw horses for the activity. Jill reminded me recently that her class set the record for the most logs debarked as somewhere around 13. I'm sure there was lots of taking turns and cheering on of classmates to accomplish that feat. Jill still comes to the farm occasionally and hosts campfires for members and friends of the foundation.

Other adventures unfolded more naturally at the farm. Sil and Ed Pembleton, who lived across the street from the farm in the Kenah home, started something called the "spur of the moment" natural phenomena hotline. One early August evening on a moment's notice, 22 adventurous Accokeekians met at 9:00 pm for a jack-o-lantern party. In this instance the jack-o-lanterns (Omphalotus olearius) were an orange to yellow mushroom with a convex cap which is a species of fungus that glows in the dark. A large colony of this fungus was growing at the base of an old stump in the barnyard. We gathered that night in the dark to see the pale green glowing gills put on a show. It was beautiful but unfortunately hard to photograph and share. Nonetheless the evening was a glowing success.

There were early morning bird walks, nighttime stargazing, and smaller but just as wonderful sightings to share with each other. These excursions allowed us to expand our ability to interpret the place for others. We were on a mission to improve the farm and its program and it was also an excuse to play, to try new things, and to see new places. We had lots of fun. In truth we were friends as well as co-workers and we liked sharing adventures at the farm and visits to other environmental centers.

The Vermont trip was one of many field trips we took to learn how other places conveyed their message to school children. It was also one of the most distant places we visited. Other trips were to Williamsburg to see a farm tool collection, Harpers Ferry to watch the magic of a technique known as living history, and the Chesapeake Bay to participate in bay restoration activities. Sil had chosen Shelburne Farms in Vermont as it was famous for its education

top: Erin Watts, Le Etta Townsend, Doris Sharp bottom: Eileen Watts & the author

program. We rented a van and drove in one day to our lodging at "Charlotte's Web Bed and Breakfast". There were six of us who could manage to leave for a week to take part in their teacher training program. We were curious as to how Shelburne Farms teacher workshops differed from ours. Days were spent touring the facility and then taking part in specially designed activities that were for students in elementary school.

Some of the more memorable activities were the maple sugaring, and dairy project where we watched cheese making. Shelburne was larger in scope, and the things they taught were specific to their site and climate. However, we gained knowledge from our interactions with other workshop participants and staff. One of the many other sites we visited in the Burlington area was a Vermont blueberry farm. In a photo taken that day, we are gathered around the bushes laden with plump and juicy blueberries. We each had buckets tied to our waist so we could pick with both hands. It took no time at all to fill the buckets. Pickers at this "pick your own" farm were not supposed to eat before weighing the bounty, but it was difficult not to sample – and we cheated. We also purchased and transported crates of blueberries back home.

At other sites like The Shelburne Museum we saw many exhibits of Vermont agricultural and cultural history. At the Ben and Jerry's Ice Cream factory we watched as workers turned cream into a commercially popular product and then we tasted extraordinary ice cream flavors like chunky monkey. At those places we were only spectators and not engaged in activities that would build lasting memories or a reference bank for future learning. However, the trip reinforced within us the knowledge that the driving element in Hard Bargain's education program must be "hands on" so that the whole experience would be one of adventure and discovery.

When I think of the Vermont trip I can still taste and feel the sweet berries exploding in my mouth. These small moments and adventures with staff, foundation members, students and visitors became big in the way we approached teaching and learning. It assured continued "Good Times at Hard Bargain". Sil was always curious to find out what our visitors were learning. In 1995 she created a board for student comments which were jotted down on post-it notes. It was a simple but effective way to get feedback. Here's a sample that tells our story.

Kid's Comments --misspelling & all!

What did you do today that you never thought you would do?

...make a pig's bed

...walk in mud and water and not get yelled at

...pet a bull. I felt adventurous. I felt alive.

...I touched a muddy crayfish and I also touched a baby pig's nose.

Write down one new thing you learned today.

... that there are a lot of animal homes everywhere.

...I never knew that the Potomac River was so big.

...I learned that cows have 4 stomachs and how small tadpoles are.

...I learned that only girl cows give milk

...I learned that turnips taste great!

The thing I will always remember about my trip to Hard Bargain Farm is...

...that animals don't harm you.

...that if you work as a team you can do anything

...I will always remember milking the cow and fishing crayfish out of the mud.

...going fishing in the swamp.

...petting the big pig. It felt like a brush.

...that it is fun and they have got some nice teachers there.

What will you do differently because of what you learned here?

...I will not throw trash on the ground when I have a family picnic.

...I will not dump liquid down the suwers anymore because I have seen what it has done to the Potomac River.

...from now on I will turn off the TV when I'm not watching it.

...I will learn to do teamwork better and to get along friendlier.

...I will treat animal s better.

...I will not pollute the Potomac River by cutting down on car rides [to reduce acid rain].

...I will never litter again. I promise.

I think Henry Ferguson would approve.

Henry Gardiner Ferguson

Sil Pembleton, Hank Xander, Le Etta Townsend, Eileen Watts, the author & Doris Sharp

EPILOGUE

Though it seems like yesterday, 20 years have passed since my retirement from Hard Bargain and it still holds a very special place in my heart. Six years ago I began recording memories of my years there and as I wrote I found myself thinking how nice it would be if Alice could know of all the wonderful and fun things that had taken place following her purchase of an old dilapidated farmhouse on the shores of the Potomac River almost 100 years ago!

We know from her writings that she wanted a place in the country, and that she loved growing things on the land, being an artist, and gathering on the river with friends to enjoy good times. She did much more than that, but I doubt for example that she ever expected to 'employ a village' in the hope of saving the community that was beginning to emerge! In 1922, it was not typical for a woman of her time to take these bold steps.

My twenty years working as executive director of Hard Bargain represent a wonderful experience of working with my neighbors and I am very grateful for the help they gave to me and to the Foundation staff as we guided the educational program and so much more.

Belva Jensen, former President of the Foundation, said it perfectly in her 1985 Annual Report to the membership:

> *"We are all so fortunate to be part of this foundation and to contribute to its success. We are unique! Everyone who works here, studies here, plays here or just visits claim a piece of this land and it's view forever. All of us share a priceless heritage preserved and left to us by Alice and Henry Ferguson. We must not fail to leave our mark on the next generation as selflessly as they did."*

Today I am a new member of the foundation's board of directors, still living in the Moyaone and looking forward to new adventures. It's amazing to me how the foundation's educational program has expanded and I believe we must continue to help it thrive. I hope you will join me in that endeavor.

Here, at the end of my story, I once again thank Alice Ferguson for saving Hard Bargain and for creating a community that cares about the land. I really did write (many) letters to Alice.

Here's a special one for you to ponder....

Alice Lescinska Lowe Ferguson

A Special Letter to Alice

Dear Alice,

Accokeek has become a magnet for people who longed for country living and could come together in community for fun and being close to the earth. The Moyaone community now encompasses a national park of more than 4000 acres. At your death there were 10 residents and 30 landowners. Now there are hundreds of residents and about 120 five-acre parcels.

It's an active place. We have unique homes, each nestled on five acres, as you and Henry envisioned. We come together at the community center for parties, maintain gardens, swim in the pool, clean the Potomac shoreline, watch performances at the amphitheater and help raise money to support two Foundations - the Alice Ferguson Foundation at your beloved Hard Bargain and the Accokeek Foundation at the National Colonial Farm at Bryans Point.

Why did we dare to settle here? Well, Tom and I wanted a country home as I believe most Moyaone residents do and we were delighted with our purchase from the beginning. As time passed and we learned more about you and Henry, and your beginnings here, and as we began to enjoy many facets of what you two had created, we became more delighted! You showed us the fun of Hard Bargain adventures, you made your home a welcoming place and a center for launching dreams, you supported each person's endeavors, and you were playful. Those who followed you, and those who continue to follow enjoy the benefits of your creation.

Thank you, Alice! You Rock!!
Sincerely,

Kay Powell

ACKNOWLEDGEMENTS

Writing this book has been a process of self-discovery. I began writing six years ago in 2012, and, in true Kay style, I knew should prepare so I enrolled in a memoir-writing class at a senior center in Annapolis. Weekly writing assignments shared with others in the class launched the project of telling my story. Later, as progress on my book stalled, I sought assistance for more extensive writing sessions from two special friends, author and coach Carol Burbank, and writer and artist Patrise Henkel.

Shortly after that, the three of us met with my friend Kay Whittington to discuss the possibility and hope of starting our own writers' group. We had the interest of several others but we needed a place to meet. Kay W. spoke with her friend Anne Ramsey, Manager of the Accokeek Branch Library, who enthusiastically endorsed our proposed plan and who ultimately arranged for us to have a meeting room in the Library on the second Monday of each month. And so, AWWG (Accokeek Women's Writers Group) was born! We started with six members... today we host more than 40 women writers - still on the second Monday of each month! These women are among the many who have cheered me on in my venture and I am so grateful to them.

Also, at the insistence of Patrise Henkel I spent one November participating in NANOWRIMO (National Novel Writers' Month) which proved to be quite helpful in my effort to gather good raw material for my book. The object of this venture is to write a small novel - about 50,000 words - in one month. It was a hoot as I met with other writers at coffee shops and we set timers and just poured words onto pages. I managed 26,000 words as I recalled my 20-year adventure at Hard Bargain.

Rereading newsletters,annual reports, new clippings, and looking at old photos was a journey into the past for me giving me a chance to reframe the hard parts of managing a small foundation. I'm especially thankful to Kay Whittington, a friend of 30 years. She was my primary editor and devoted time weekly to review drafts and to make my stories more entertaining as well as grammatically correct.

Carol Burbank, through Storyweaving Coaching encouraged me with private sessions and workshops. Patrise Henkel created the cover design, sorted through photos, and laid out the book using her wealth and talent as an artist and writer. Mary Keifer graciously offered her professional editing skills. Charlotte Gillespie, Le Etta Townsend and Doris Sharp, friends for many years, read drafts and gave me much helpful feedback

There are so many folks to thank... six years of friends who have so often graciously listened to and answered my questions. To you all - sincere gratitude.

Many thanks also to the Alice Ferguson Foundation for their generous use of archival photos and documents. Finally, grateful thanks to my husband, Tom Powell, who encouraged me all along the way and patiently endured my many absences. And sometimes I think I might have titled this memoir Thank you Alice.

Board Presidents who I was priveleged to serve under:

Louis Sandine	1976-1980
Elmer S. Biles	1980-1984
Belva L. Jensen	1984-1986
Caroline Beane	1986-1990
Martha Mills	1990-1994
Joseph DeStefanis	1994-1998
Jean Thompson	1998-2002

CPSIA information can be obtained
at www.ICGtesting.com
Printed in the USA
JSHW020845081219
2828JS00004B/15

9 781734 264401